D1044988

WHAT OTHERS ARE SAYING

"Dreamers are a dime a dozen; it's the doers that change the world! If you're ready to stop simply dreaming and start turning your dreams into action, then Next will show you the way."

—DAVE RAMSEY
New York Times best-selling author
and nationally syndicated radio show host

"Every day we see the products of dreams. Telephones, airplanes, skyscrapers, Disney World ... All the mental architects responsible for these discoveries and innovations have one thing in common—they actively and passionately pursued their dreams.

"In his motivating new book, *Next*, Adonis inspires us all to action. I challenge you to read this book, then take inventory of your dreams and goals and not let another day pass without moving forward."

—DAVE MARTIN
America's #1 Christian success coach and best-selling author

"Are you stuck in self-doubt? Frozen by fear? Is hesitation clouding your destination? Adonis will take you from breakdown to breakthrough with his practical advice, guidance, and step-by-step plan for unlocking your potential. If you're ready for your next level, *Next* is the book for you!"

—MANDY HALE
New York Times best-selling author of *I've Never Been to Vegas but My Luggage Has* and chief blogger at *The Single Woman*

"This unique book covers the full spectrum of self-improvement and self-analysis. Its down-to-earth, practical style makes it easy for the reader to apply what's in the book to their individual lives, no matter what stage they are in. *Next* is filled with encouragement, motivation, and inspiration that will empower you to reach for your dreams once again."

—DR. RON KELLEY
CEO at National School Improvement Corporation and international motivational speaker and author

"*Next* is a fantastic book with real-world advice anyone can implement immediately—and should! Adonis does a stellar job giving step-by-step instructions on how to achieve your Next, no matter who you are, where you are, or what your Next is. If you aren't living to your fullest potential, or haven't reached your dreams and know there's something more for you, there is finally help! I can only imagine the success stories that will come from reading this encouraging and inspiring book, and I look forward to hearing how its message impacts readers!"

—MICHELLE MOORE
Award-winning author and speaker, leadership coach

"Every dreamer reaches a place where they have to face what's holding them back and either let their dream die or answer the call—to take the leap of faith and go forward. *Next* is the perfect book that will keep you from settling for less than what you dream about, and inspire and motivate you to make those dreams a reality."

—CHRIS LOCURTO
Entrepreneur, leadership and business coach, CEO of The Poimen Group

"In this inspiring and motivational book, Adonis provides practical steps to take you from where you are to where you want to be. He will help you overcome the challenge of getting stuck in your past on your way to your future. This book will enable you to move to your Next, now! I highly recommend it!"

—MIKE RADCLIFFE
Lead pastor at Destiny Church, UK

"One of my favorite speakers and leaders, Adonis Lenzy, has created a powerful resource for helping us fulfill our dreams. The passion and practicality in this book are second to none. By using this valuable book as a roadmap to success, you'll find that your Next is closer than you think!"

—RONNIE DOSS
Author, speaker, and leadership trainer

"As an eleven-year-old kid growing up in Brooklyn, New York, I fell in love with basketball and dreamed about playing in the NBA. Along the way I learned that hard work beats talent when talent doesn't work hard. So I made sure I worked as hard as I could to match the talent I was given. Every dream requires hard work and dedication, and *Next* will definitely be a resource of motivation and inspiration to keep you moving forward."

—CHRIS TAFT
Former NBA power forward-center
for the Golden State Warriors

Next

*What to Do When
You Know There's
Something More*

ADONIS LENZY

BroadStreet
PUBLISHING

BroadStreet Publishing Group, LLC
Racine, Wisconsin, USA
www.broadstreetpublishing.com

Next

What to Do When You Know There's Something More

Copyright © 2015 Adonis Lenzy

ISBN: 978-1-4245-5105-7 (hardcover)
ISBN: 978-1-4245-5106-4 (e-book)

All rights reserved. No part of this book may be reproduced in any form, except for brief quotations in printed reviews, without permission in writing from the publisher.

Cover design by Chris Garborg at www.garborgdesignworks.com
Interior by Katherine Lloyd at www.TheDESKonline.com
Edited by Alice Sullivan at www.alicesullivan.com

Printed in China
15 16 17 18 19 20 5 4 3 2 1

This book is dedicated to my wife, Heather,
and two children, Grayson and Kherington.
God has truly blessed me with an amazing family,
and doing life with them always inspires me
to be the best that I can be.

CONTENTS

PART I
IT STINKS TO BE STUCK

PART II
SO WHAT'S NEXT?

PART III
FACING FEAR HEAD-ON

PART IV
INCREASING YOUR CAPACITY

PART V
MAKE YOUR NEXT DAYS YOUR BEST DAYS

PREFACE

S ometimes in life we find ourselves still dreaming the dream but not living the dream. We reach a place called "Stuck," which has the potential to lead to discouragement and unhappiness. We do the same old mundane activities at the workplace, school, or home while constantly dreaming about and imagining the life we really want to lead.

Some of us have even reached our big dream or goal in life and have been quite successful. Then over the course of time, a new dream emerges and we are no longer satisfied with our current success; this new desire begins to push us to attain the next thing for our life.

The purpose of this book is to show people how to manage the emotions of their current situation and encourage and equip them to take strategic next steps toward their dreams. Anyone can apply these actions and ideas to his or her life. My hope is that in doing so, readers will find the motivation to pursue their dreams once again.

FOREWORD

by Danny Gokey

American Idol *finalist, artist, entertainer,*
and founder of Sophia's Heart

When my first wife, Sophia, and I decided that we were going to try out for *American Idol*, little did I know that I would lose her one month before the audition. Her passing away was devastating. I didn't want to do the audition; I was just trying to figure out how to live at that moment. Pushing myself through a devastating time in my life and taking those next steps eventually led to me living the dream that was in our hearts. Now my story of hope is helping others around the world to reach their dreams and never give up.

The principles and practical steps in this book are some of the same that I had to apply to my life in order to move forward. For anyone who has been feeling stuck, discouraged, or in a rut, this book will challenge you to take some necessary action steps that will cause you to start gaining traction and moving your life in a positive direction. You will be inspired, encouraged, and motivated to go after those dreams and make them your reality. There is hope in front of you, and your success all depends on what you do *Next*.

INTRODUCTION

"Men are often capable of greater things than they perform. They are sent into the world with bills of credit, and seldom draw to their full extent."

—*Horace Walpole*

f you picked up this book, it's likely because you, like many people around the world, are tired of being stuck where you are while only dreaming about where you want to be. You may even be skeptical. Perhaps you've already read several motivational books but still feel like you're in the same place doing the same old thing. If that sounds familiar, you're not alone.

Self-help or motivational books often leave me thinking that my next step is so far out of my reach that it is unattainable. Some also leave me feeling as if I have to be an expert or a professional before I can accomplish what the book is telling me to do. At the end of books like these, I often feel overwhelmed just thinking about the information and exhausted before even putting one principle into practice. Instead of being motivated to conquer the world, I feel insecure and unsure about myself, my dream, and my ability to make it happen. Chances are, you may have felt this way a time or two yourself. And that's why this book is intentionally different!

Next is designed for the everyday person like you and me. It's designed for the dreamer who is not an expert but is ready to start making accomplishments in his or her life. There are practical steps that anybody can implement if they will just put forth a little bit of effort. The content is not overwhelming and it won't leave your head spinning for hours. The information can help get you going in the right direction if you begin to apply it to your daily life.

Yes, you'll have to do a little bit of work—but think about how much work you already do each day to either maintain or fight against your current situation! I'm not asking you to find an extra three hours each day to focus on your next steps; I'm only asking you to channel your energy, efforts, and thoughts in a different direction.

Anything will work if *you work it.*

⊰ • ⊱

Maybe you're sick and tired of waking up on Monday morning dreading the drive to a job that is sucking the very life right out of you. You've been dreaming of something more. You know there's something more. You just don't know what steps to take to get there.

Or like many people, perhaps you once loved your job but you've reached a place where the passion is no longer there. At one time you were excited about the job and even its mundane activities. You were fulfilled on a daily basis, and your enthusiasm was quite evident. And then it happened. Not all of a sudden but year by year, month by month, week by week, and day by day, your passion, desire, enthusiasm, and fulfillment slowly turned into frustration or disinterest. You soon found yourself dreading each new week, having to motivate yourself in the morning just to get out of bed and drive to work. Then you watch the clock every day, counting down the hours until you get to go home and relax … until the next day.

That's not a fun place to be in. Trust me, I've been there a time or two in my life—where I was stuck, discouraged, and desperately looking for a ray of hope or a glimpse of the future that I had been dreaming about for years. One thing I realized is that the longer you stay in that rut, the worse it gets for you and others around you.

When I was in my late twenties and in between jobs, my savings account was being drained by the month and signs of depression began to appear. There were times I didn't even want to get out of bed or face another day. I didn't want to be around other people, either, for fear of them asking me, "So what have you been up to lately?" I didn't want to have to tell people about my lack of a job and lack of direction.

I got so wrapped up in the negatives that I almost quit dreaming about a brighter future for myself. Then all of a sudden it hit me! You can call it a revelation or an epiphany, but whatever it was, it caused a drastic shift in my thinking. I went from feeling like a complete failure and a worthless human being to having more positive thoughts. I found myself thinking, "Wait a minute … my life is not that bad, and I've made some big accomplishments already!"

I realized I was having one of the biggest pity parties of my life! I was fixating on a temporary setback and moment of failure instead of celebrating the major steps that I had already taken in my life. Once I realized that much, I began to encourage myself by remembering the good moments on my journey and the accomplishments of all my previous goals. I knew that my life wasn't over. I still had many more things to do with my life, even though it was difficult to see in that moment. Dreaming beyond my current situation and circumstances was the key to getting me back on track—and it will be transformational to your life as well, once you begin to focus on all of the positives, not the negatives.

Whether you realize it or not, you have the power and ability to change your life and your future anytime you want. All you have to do is figure out the next steps to take. I made a decision to stay stuck no longer, and you can make that decision too.

Sometimes people are afraid to go after their dreams because of numerous failed attempts in their past. Feelings of failure and disappointment, if not properly handled, have the potential to stop you from ever trying again. However, my hope is that something in one of these chapters—a word of encouragement, a real-life example, or a nugget of new information—will ignite a spark inside you that will energize you and stir up the passion and desire to reach for those dreams once again.

Dare to dream again.

It's time for you to grab those dreams off the shelf and out of the corners of your mind. It's time to dust them off and start dreaming about them with the same fire and passion you once did.

Dare to believe again.

It's time to believe in your dream and in yourself once again. You must believe that no matter what, *you will make it*. You must believe that you will reach your dreams and accomplish what others think is impossible. You must hold on to your belief with a tenacity that will endure anything that comes your way.

Dare to hope again.

Most people don't hope for the best because they are focused on the worst that could happen. But I'm here to tell you that you must hold on to the hope of a better tomorrow. Fix your eyes and your thoughts on the hope of a bright future.

⊰ • ⊱

If you've found yourself stuck in an area of life, this book will be a step in the right direction. If you're already on the way to your dream, this book will serve as an inspiration and motivator for you to keep moving forward. Even if you have reached one of your big goals, you must ask yourself, "What's next?"

My guess is that regardless of where you are, who you are, or the circumstances you're encountering right now, you sense a shift in your near future—even if it feels like the slightest internal whisper that there's more for you to do—and you are ready to go to the next level.

As you read through the chapters of this book, you will be inspired, encouraged, motivated, and empowered to go after those wild, far-fetched dreams—even the ones that others told you were impossible to obtain. Even the ones *you told yourself* were impossible to attain.

Big dreams benefit a lot of people beyond just the one who dreams them. Chances are, by reaching your dream you will enable others to reach theirs.

It's up to you to take the next steps that will move you forward. The key to your success all depends on what you do *Next*.

Are you ready?

On your mark, get set, *go*!

PART I

IT STINKS
TO BE STUCK

One of the worst feelings in the world is being stuck in traffic when you are trying to get somewhere. It's frustrating, aggravating, and irritating, even to the mildest-tempered person. To be perfectly honest, I can't think of anyone who enjoys sitting in traffic. It's usually a time that brings out the worst in humanity—especially in our language and behavior!

Apply that scenario to other parts of life, and the results are eerily similar.

People are on their way somewhere every day. Some are repeating the same actions every day; some are trying to reach a dream they have been aiming at for quite some time. Then it happens. They hit a moment of standstill, sitting idle on the road, and they feel as if they aren't going anywhere or making any progress.

They are no longer gaining any traction.

Momentum has slowed or stopped altogether.

Anger begins to set in.

The panic button is triggered by the thought of missing their moment of opportunity.

Then it happens—road rage!

It happens to everyone at one time or another. The keys to moving forward are to acknowledge it, assess the situation, and then work on a new path to becoming unstuck!

There is no greater feeling than seeing the traffic jam ahead clear and the cars slowly beginning to move.

Chapter 1

WHEN EVERY DAY FEELS LIKE MONDAY

Do you feel an overwhelming sense of discouragement as your weekend is winding down and coming to a close? Do thoughts of Monday morning and starting another workweek begin to haunt you as early as Saturday afternoon? Maybe you've been doing the same old thing year after year and your workweek has become more like the movie *Groundhog Day*. It's a funny film. But living this way is anything but fun.

Bill Murray is a weatherman sent to cover a story about a weather-forecasting groundhog. He's covered the same story four times and is absolutely miserable about doing it again, but he does, since his job is to cover Groundhog Day. To his surprise when he wakes up the next morning, it is Groundhog Day all over again! He's forced to live the same day over and over again until he learns to break the cycles of boredom and frustration.

I once saw an alarming statistic that nearly 80 percent of people have reported getting what is commonly known as the *Sunday night blues.** And a whopping 62 percent said they get it "really

---

* Business Wire, "Sunday Night Blues: The Dread of Workers Everywhere," Monster, October 7, 2013, http://www.monster.com/about/a/1072013-D3126728.

bad." In the United States that number jumped to 76 percent.[*] This condition is characterized by anxiety about the week ahead and a sense of helplessness and depression. It most often occurs on Sunday afternoons and evenings, but it can start as early as Friday after work! When people start thinking about all their responsibilities and deadlines, this has a tendency to bring on unhealthy levels of stress.

I think it's fair to state that even when people love their jobs, they still may be prone to catching a case of the *Sunday night blues* every now and then. Fortunately for them, since they love what they do, they can usually reconcile their stresses toward the end of their workweek and better prepare for Monday morning, ultimately reducing stress in advance.

But let's look at it from the perspective of those who are constantly frustrated and no longer enjoy where they are in life, nor what they are doing. In this situation, the Sunday night blues can be a very real phenomenon. The thought of Monday morning has haunted these folks since their weekend began, and instead of relaxing and thinking of all the ways they can overcome the blues, their thoughts are consumed with how to avoid the blues altogether—in essence, they're running from the situation because they can't stand it any longer. They might consider calling in sick or taking a vacation day because they don't have the mental or physical strength to go through the motions at work. If these people aren't careful, they will focus too much on the misery they are in and eventually end up on a downward spiral into the pit of despair.

---

[*] "Red, White and Mostly Blue: Monster Data Shows that the US Continues to Suffer the Most from Sunday Night Blues," Monster, June 2, 2015, http://www.monster.com/about/a/Red-White-and-Mostly-Blue-Monster-Data-Shows-that-the-US-Continues-to-Suffer-the-Most-from-Sunday-Night-Blues.

They will focus too much on what is instead of focusing on what could be. It is even possible to generate so much stress over the situation that the person literally makes himself or herself ill!

If you're in this situation, there is hope. *There is always hope.* The Sunday night blues very well may be an indicator that there is something else out there for you—and what you're doing right now isn't what you were meant to do. There's likely a position, calling, or career that has the potential to bring you the joy, excitement, and fulfillment you have been longing for. You just haven't discovered it yet!

So now that you've considered the possibility that there's something else out there for you, here's a little exercise to help you combat those Sunday night blues.

STEP ONE:

1. Take a moment to write out a list of activities and/or emotions that have a tendency to put you in the *Sunday night blues* mood.

2. Think about how you feel in that moment, and also think about how you *respond* to that feeling. Do you lose energy and drive? Do you think of ways to escape the situation entirely, such as calling in sick? This requires honesty on your part.

STEP TWO:

Now that you've been honest with yourself, you've probably pinpointed a few activities that automatically make you shut down or become defensive. Now we can counteract that with a different kind of activity and/or emotion.

1. Take a moment to write down an activity that will counteract each of the activities or combat the emotions on your list in step one. For example, if one of your items was that you begin to feel an overwhelming sadness and depression as your weekend comes to a close, then a next step could be planning activities that are fun, exhilarating, and exciting for you to do. It could be something as simple as watching a comedy show.

2. Make sure you make time for these new activities in your schedule!

Chapter 2

AM I THERE YET?

S o there I was, standing in one of the longest lines I had ever been in at the Department of Motor Vehicles because it was time to renew my tags. I'm sure you've been there too. I'd almost rather be at the dentist getting a root canal than standing in a line at the DMV! At least the dentist gives you pain medication.

As I impatiently checked the time every minute, it was evident that I was in for a long and unpleasant time. I began to look at the other people in line. I saw people by themselves who displayed the same frustrations as I did. I also saw a few married couples, their hands filled with paperwork, irritated at the process and hoping they had the right paperwork with them.

I was in a place I didn't want to be, with people that I didn't even know, and I felt as if my life were wasting away every minute of the hour. I realized I was in a room with more than one hundred people from all walks of life, ethnic diversities, and backgrounds. The one thing we had in common was that we did not want to be there. And then it happened—someone at the counter said "next" and caused the entire line to take a step forward. Just the mere power of that word, spoken by a total stranger, caused me to change my attitude with every step I took.

I felt a sense of hope that my time would come and I would be out of there soon.

> Just the mere power of the word Next
> caused me to change my attitude with every step I took.

Each time the word was called out, the line shifted and some-one made it to their destination. The closer I got to the service window, the more encouraged I became. I kept moving forward until I was the next one in line. What a great feeling it was to be there and ready to accomplish my goal!

Let's face it—we all want to get to our dreams as soon as pos-sible. The reality is, success doesn't happen overnight, and if you could accomplish your dream in one day, then it's not much of a dream anyhow. If your dream is big, it will take time. You will have to learn to be patient.

The Patience of a Child

My wife and I have two small children, and we have learned that if a close friend or family member is coming to visit, we'd better wait to tell our kids that they are coming until two or three days before they arrive. The reason we do this is because our kids will continue to ask us several times a day when so-and-so will be here. They eventually sound like little broken records, repeating the same thing over and over. You see, kids are not that patient; when they get something in their minds, they want it now. Telling them about the guests a few days before they arrive gives us lever-age when it comes to setting our expectations for their behavior during the visit. We have a few days to set the tone with them.

But as an adult, you must have a different behavior and

mind-set. Your goal will not be reached overnight. You might feel stressed out about your current circumstances or situation. You may be tired of waiting for your turn to be next or tired of the overwhelming feeling of being stuck.

My encouragement to you today is that this too shall pass. Nothing lasts forever, and that includes your feelings of discomfort. If they are temporary, then they are subject to change and you can start changing them now.

The good news is: if you are stuck, then at least you know where you are and from there you can begin to devise a plan that will get you unstuck and back on your way to reaching for your dreams. You first have to make the decision that you are sick and tired of being stuck and you are ready to do something about it. Then you have to take action.

Being stuck is a choice.

It's Driving Me Crazy

Call it being unsettled. Call it a gut feeling. Whatever you call it—you know it is your body's way of telling you to pay attention to your current situation. With these internal signals, your body can keep you safe from harmful situations or people. It can also alert you when you're unfulfilled by giving you a sense of longing or the feeling that you should be doing more.

In the movie *The Lion King*, Mufasa tells young Simba, "You are more than what you have become." It is a profound statement in a heartwarming kids' movie, but it applies to us all, especially when we feel like we've lost traction. If this sounds like your current situation, don't panic—it doesn't mean you are behind schedule or that you have wasted years of your life in Settleville. (This is a place in life where people settle for less than what they could be doing. We'll talk more about Settleville a little later in the book.) But for now, just know that oftentimes these internal pushes are indicators that something is about to shift in your life and move you into the next thing.

When you ignore that small voice inside of you that is calling you to move forward toward your dreams, it grows weaker. But the longer you ignore it, the more your feelings of being stuck will intensify. You will become easily agitated and irritated. Your coworkers will not want to be around you. Your family members will know that something is wrong. Before long, you will begin to beat yourself up—arguing with yourself over the action you should take.

Trust me: at this point, the thought of wanting more is not going to go away. It will follow you. You won't be able to escape it. It will be waiting on you as you clock out from a long day at work with mandatory overtime. It will be with you as you head to your car, walking across a dark, deserted parking lot. It will echo in your mind that there is more for you than what you are experiencing right now. That voice will confront you while you're driving, during your quiet times, and even in the shower. It will challenge you and leave you face-to-face with a decision that could change your life forever.

The question is, are you going to embrace the voice—the internal push—this time? Or are you going to ignore it until tomorrow and go through the battle all over again?

You can *have* more. You can *do* more. You can *live the life* that you've dreamed of.

While in line at the Department of Motor Vehicles that day, it only took a small step to move my journey forward. Likewise, the path to your dream only requires you to take a single step forward at a time.

Whether you've been waiting for a long time for your dream to happen, or you've just discovered your dream—it is never too late or too early to take the next step. Your moment of opportunity has not passed you by. Don't listen to the lies—believe the truth instead: it's never too late to make your next days your best days.

Chapter 3

MIND
MONSTERS

During times of uncertainty, a plethora of thoughts can bombard you until you're in an all-out battle of the mind. You may think, "By now I should be farther along in my career." You may also think, "By now I should be financially stable." Or maybe, "By now I should be married." Fear of missing out creeps into our minds, and we feel like we're quickly running out of time to accomplish the goal or reach the dream. Our dream that once brought a fire and passion to us is now being challenged by the nightmare of never living the life we dream about, thanks to the Mind Monsters.

So what can we do?

Well, one of the easiest and fastest ways to break free from the Mind Monsters is to simply take a step back from your situation and change your perspective.

Midair Mind Monsters

When my son Grayson was one year old, we traveled to Wisconsin to visit family. This was the first plane trip that my wife and I took with him, and we were both a little nervous. We didn't want to have a screaming child on the plane and be "those parents with that kid." The flight to Wisconsin was very smooth and our son was awesome—so awesome that we received many compliments on how well he was doing on the plane. We were proud parents. Then came the flight back home to Nashville after our vacation.

The flight was a little delayed, and Grayson was starting to get antsy from being stuck in the terminal. When the plane finally arrived, we were excited to board and get home. Unfortunately there was bad weather in the area, and the pilot came over the intercom to inform us that we were grounded until further notice.

For the next few hours, we were stuck on the plane on the runway with a one-year-old. It was hot, and he was getting irritated. While Grayson did relatively well, the Mind Monsters started having a ball with some of the passengers. They started getting annoyed with each other and began to make rude comments about those that boarded the plane late, as if it were their fault we didn't take off in time.

Tempers started flaring. Nasty remarks were being thrown at the flight attendants left and right. People were upset about missing their connecting flights and complaining about how the airline had messed up all of their plans. One person even called the airline's customer service department from the plane and demanded a refund. It was a scene right out of the movies. To make matters even worse, one passenger went to the bathroom on the plane and the smell was awful.

Finally, after three hours of sitting on the plane, we were cleared for takeoff.

My wife and I were thrilled that we were finally going home. We were also thrilled that the tension on the plane finally settled and everyone seemed a lot happier than before.

I learned a few things that day about perspective. Some people had the perception that they were stuck on a plane and it was the airline's fault. Therefore, attitudes and tempers flared out of control. One guy was so rude and obnoxious to the attendants that I wanted to turn around and give him a piece of my mind, but my wife talked me out of it.

In the beginning I admit that I was just as irritated as the next person. I felt trapped on a plane with no way out. But then something happened. I noticed that my son was doing fine and enjoying himself. When it got too hot on the plane, we stripped him down to a T-shirt and his diaper and let him crawl the aisle. He was very happy and entertaining to everyone close by. I looked out the window and saw the dark clouds and lightning, which we were avoiding by staying grounded for our safety. I then realized that I wasn't stuck; I was being protected from what could have been a dangerous situation for my family and me. My perspective changed everything. It changed my attitude and my demeanor. I overcame the Mind Monsters.

You may not necessarily be stuck on a plane in the middle of the runway, but you may feel that you are stuck in a job or a routine that has brought an overwhelming sense of dissatisfaction. You could become angry at those around you for no reason at all. And you could easily become short tempered with your spouse and children. You may be unpleasant to be around at work or in your free time and not even know it!

Don't believe me? Here are two examples of how those ugly Mind Monsters tend to work in daily life.

Trouble in Paradise

When my wife and I got married, we went to St. Lucia for our honeymoon. We were having a great time until my wife decided she wanted to go kayaking. Some people think that I have a water phobia because of my dislike for the ocean. It's not the ocean that bothers me; it's what's *in* the ocean—*I have a shark phobia.* Nevertheless, she wanted to go kayaking, and as much as I fought the idea, we ended up going anyway.

I thought I could handle it. I thought we'd just paddle out a few yards and turn around. But that didn't happen. She wanted to go out farther, and we ended up about two hundred yards from the shore. All I could think about was sharks, and that's when the Mind Monsters took over.

As I began to get angry, the Mind Monsters began to paint a clear picture in my mind of what was going to happen: In less than two minutes the whole scenario ran through my mind—a shark was going to come and bump the kayak, knocking us into the water. The shark was going to eat my wife and I would be the survivor, only to later be accused of murdering my wife at sea. It would be her fault that I was going to spend the rest of my life in prison for a crime I didn't commit! All because she wanted to go kayaking.

So there I was on my honeymoon, in a beautiful location, angry at my wife for no good reason. Thankfully I realized that I was allowing my thoughts to take over and that I should be enjoying our honeymoon. I also learned an important lesson about marriage dynamics: "Happy wife equals happy life."

Assuming the Worst

Here's another example that may be more familiar to you. Imagine you're at work early one Friday morning and as you pass by two coworkers, they are having one of those whispering conversations. When you walk by, they get really quiet as they quickly glance at you and only make brief eye contact.

You walk back to your desk, trying to figure out what the heck that was all about. Before long you conclude that they must have been gossiping about you. After all, they got quiet and couldn't look you in the eyes when you walked by. Did you do something wrong? Are you about to be fired? Maybe they are trying to sabotage your chance of getting that promotion you've been wanting for a while.

You can't even work effectively for the rest of the day because you are spying on them and eavesdropping on any nearby conversation. You are sure they are saying bad things about you, spreading lies to get you in trouble with the boss. Your day is ruined and your mind is bombarded with negative thoughts toward them.

Then after lunch, those same two coworkers come into your office with smiles on their faces; one is carrying a gift bag and the other is holding a huge cupcake with a candle in it. You see, today is Friday and they know that your birthday is Sunday, so they wanted to surprise you with an early birthday celebration! You are confused, shocked, excited, relieved—and you feel like a complete idiot—all at the same time. Those Mind Monsters nearly turned your surprise birthday celebration into a disaster.

Move Over, Mind Monsters!

The Mind Monsters' main job is to keep you discouraged and at a standstill by consuming your thoughts with fears, excuses, and negative emotions. The Mind Monsters will try to convince you that it's too late or that you are too old to do what you've always wanted to do. They will taunt your mind with thoughts of inadequacy and insecurity. They'll convince you that other people are out to get you.

There's an old saying that goes, "Whatever happens in your

mind will happen in time." If your mind tells you that you're stuck, then chances are your entire being will listen and follow its suggestions. Being stuck in an old mind-set or pattern of thought is more mental than it is physical. If what you are currently doing is not working for you, then you might need to make some adjustments to get back on track and on your way to accomplishing your dreams and goals.

Maybe you're not stuck at all and it's just not the right timing for you to proceed; nevertheless, you still perceive it as being stuck. If that's the case, perhaps all you need to do right now is change your perception on your circumstances.

Take a deep breath. Look around. And try to see your situation from a different—and positive!—perspective.

The Madness of Running Late

One day I was in a hurry to get somewhere and wouldn't you know it, I found myself behind a slow driver on a small, two-lane road with no opportunity to pass him. He was barely moving down the road, crawling at about ten miles an hour! The Mind Monsters got the best of me and instantly I was furious. They kept whispering, "You're never going to get there on time. You're going to miss this important meeting and opportunity because of the slow driver in front of you." I'm not going to write everything I said out loud or thought about this person, but trust me—it wasn't nice. I even went so far as to blow my horn at him. I was tormented by the awful thought of missing my appointment, and it was all this ridiculous driver's fault!

Then it happened. I looked ahead, past seven or eight cars in front of me, and saw a hearse being led by two police motorcycles. That's right—I had somehow pulled into the *middle* of a funeral precession. I felt like an idiot! I wanted to crawl under a rock and hide. I can only imagine what the people in the funeral procession were thinking about me.

That funny (and unfortunate) story definitely gets a laugh every time I share it, but the truth is that we have all been in a similar situation at one time or another because we are not getting where we want to go fast enough. We get irritated and aggravated at the littlest thing. We tend to blame others for our lack of forward progress. I was blaming the car in front of me for making me late to my appointment, when I was in the wrong in the first place by somehow finding my way into a funeral procession!

It's in those moments that you must learn to control your emotions by ignoring the voices of the Mind Monsters that are trying to trip you up. They are trying to get you to respond and act out of anger, and if you heed their voices, you will no doubt delay your Next.

Chapter 4

DREAM DISTRACTIONS

It happens without fail: the moment you make up your mind to start moving toward your dreams or goals, you will invariably encounter resistance, setbacks, and failures on your journey. Now, don't freak out. These circumstances are all just a part of the process, and they will happen a time or two while you're on your journey for bigger and better. The key to your success will depend on your ability to stay focused and not get distracted. Some of these dream distractions will include circumstances you have no control over. Other dream distractions can be self-imposed, such as making excuses.

When you have a big dream, you usually want to share it with others. Sharing a dream is often done with the expectation of the other person being fully supportive. But sometimes that's just not the case. The thoughts and opinions of others, especially when they differ from your own, can serve as a deflator at times and steal your dream.

Sometimes the unsolicited advice from your friends and family has the tendency to distract you as well. Maybe they cautioned you about taking such a huge risk. Perhaps their words were laced with skepticism and doubt about your new venture. You start pondering their words over and over in your mind until you actually believe them yourself, and now you are second-guessing your whole dream.

Time can also be a dream distraction. People simply give up because they think it has taken far too long and their time to be great has simply passed.

Dream distractions have the power and the potential to keep your dreams from becoming a reality. Reaching your goals and desires in life takes a laser-like focus. Distractions are the enemy of focus and can slow your progress or stop you altogether if you place your attention on them. Avoiding distractions can keep you on task and on target. The key is learning to recognize the things or even people that are a distraction.

Manage Your Mind-set

One way to easily recognize distractions is to discern between the different kinds of interruptions. Always remember that life is filled with interruptions, but there are different levels of interruption. If something comes up and requires a little of my time and I can handle it while still staying focused on my current project, then I see it as a normal life interruption. When something happens and it totally interrupts my thought process and I am no longer able to focus any mental energy on the task at hand, then I see it as a distraction.

Once when I was speaking at a men's conference in Mobile, Alabama, I headed back to the hotel to get some rest after the morning session. I had a great message prepared and was excited to share it with the men that night. But the moment I laid my head on the pillow, the phone rang. It was my wife, and she started the conversation by saying, "I wasn't going to call you, but …" I knew that couldn't be good.

Our upstairs air-conditioning unit was out, and the repairman was quoting between $400 and $1,700 for the repair. That call quickly went from a small interruption to a huge distraction. I was no longer able to rest, nor did I have any enthusiasm about giving my message later, because my mind was distracted by a big interruption. I was busy trying to figure out whether or not the repairman was trying to rip us off, and I was anxious about having to come up with $1,700.

Then it happened—standing in the hotel room, talking with the repairman, I realized I couldn't afford to let this take my mind off the task at hand. I told him to just get the A/C unit up and running and when I got back home I would schedule a full service appointment and would replace it then, if needed. That little distraction cost me about $400 that day.

I realized it wasn't about the money, but it was all about me not being there at home to take care of the situation myself. Once I got off the phone with the repairman, I immediately felt a sense of peace. I was able to get some rest and was excited and ready for the evening session at the conference.

It's imperative that you are on the lookout for these distractions as you continue to gain speed and momentum while moving to your Next. Don't become a victim of the distractions by giving in to the impulses they trigger.

Bring Out the Blinders

Sometimes I will catch a major horse race, such as the Kentucky Derby, on television. As I watch the horses come trotting out toward the gates, they look absolutely amazing and so powerful. They are trained for speed and it's very evident. One of the things I also notice is that the horses are wearing blinders. These blinders, which are also known as blinkers, serve a distinct purpose. A horse's eyes are set on the side of their heads, which creates great peripheral vision, but can also pick up many distractions in the field of vision. The blinders are worn to eliminate as much distraction (the crowds, other horses, etc.) as possible and to help keep the horse focused on running straight ahead.

Just like a horse's blinders keep him focused, a mental picture of your dream or goal can serve as a blinder for you. By focusing on the dream, you will reduce the distractions as you move toward your vision.

People who are stuck in life have often fallen victim to the following dream distractions:

1. The Distraction of Tomorrow

When you put things off until tomorrow, they usually end up on a long list that never—or rarely—gets touched. That list usually turns into regret because you never got around to doing the things that would have helped you accomplish your goals in life.

Here's the age-old question: "Why put off till tomorrow what you can do today?" You must use every ounce of your energy today to work toward your dreams. Act as if what you do today determines your future tomorrow. Because it does!

Here are a few tips that can help you avoid the distraction of tomorrow. These can be implemented regardless of what your dream is.

a) Do something every day that is related to you reaching your dream or goal.

Don't let one day go by in which you haven't taken a step that gets you closer to your destination. Do something, lest you do nothing. Having a mental or physical checklist can help you reach this goal.

I have a dream of writing more books besides the two I've already authored, so every day I make sure that I am writing something. Whether it's a blog post or simply jotting down a few thoughts throughout the day, I make sure I am in a constant mode of writing.

b) Schedule a start and completion deadline for weekly action items.

We are great at starting but usually need a little help and motivation to actually finish what we've started. When you are serious about reaching your dream, your calendar should reflect it. We live in such a busy era; usually the things that get scheduled on our calendars are the things that actually get done.

When my wife and I speak to married couples with children, we always tell them to schedule a date night because if it doesn't get scheduled on your calendar, it probably won't happen. Once it's on your calendar, you can then set those reminders that will alert you daily that the completion date is soon approaching.

> When you are serious about reaching your dream,
> your calendar should reflect it.

c) When you finish one goal or action item, make sure you quickly replace it with a new one.

This keeps your momentum going and keeps you from slowly slacking off and becoming idle. Yes, you can take the time to celebrate yourself for completing that task and crossing it off your list. Treat yourself to your favorite dessert or take your spouse out for an evening on the town. Do whatever makes you feel celebrated, but don't throw a weeklong party only to end up with a "lazy hangover." Stay focused and stay in the game.

d) Stay ahead of the game.

It's no fun to fall behind and play catch-up all the time. For instance, I like to put out a blog post at least two times per week. The last thing I want to do is wait until the last minute to write it when it is scheduled to post the next day. I put it on my calendar for a reason: to make it a practice to start at least two days early so I am not writing under the gun and posting something in a hurry.

When I'm working on a large project, I make sure to connect in advance with all the other people that will be involved in the process. This makes them aware of my intent and progress so we will be prepared when the time comes for our individual meetings or conference calls.

2. The Distraction of Applause

Too much applause will cause you to think that you are better than you really are. If you start to think that you no longer need improvement—like you have arrived and now you know it all—you'll eventually stop challenging yourself to grow more. But nothing could be farther from the truth. Going after the applause of people will eventually cause you to become stagnant and stale in your comfortable place of mediocrity.

Some people get so energized by the excitement that others show toward their accomplishments that they get a "big head," and that's not good at all. You must always keep moving, even if you're getting great recognition, and even when your cheerleaders are no longer there to refuel and energize you.

Always remember that determination will get you to your Next—not the applause of people. Yes, it's great to have friends and family cheering you on, but there will be many times when you find yourself on a lonely road. It's then that you will have to be your own cheerleader and motivate yourself to keep going.

3. The Distraction of Comparison

Sizing yourself up to others can bring frustration and disappointment about what you don't have, and you'll fail to recognize what you do have. It's natural for us to look at someone we admire or someone who is already a success at what we want to do and think that they got there without any struggles. In truth, you have no idea what it took for them to get to where they are today. Instead of asking people about their success, ask them for their presuccess story. I'm sure it's filled with ups and downs as well as minor and major setbacks along the way. We make the biggest mistake when we only compare ourselves with their end results and not their beginnings. This leaves us weary and defeated before we even start the journey.

Don't waste any more time comparing yourself with another person. You don't have time to get caught up in that web of distraction.

> The problem with comparison is that you envision
> the other person as better than they really are.

When I first started writing and blogging, I read other people's blogs. What began as looking for ideas quickly turned to comparison as I saw how professional their blogs looked. After just a few minutes I would find myself in a full panic attack and overwhelmed by comparing my blog to theirs—and these were people who had been blogging and writing for years before I even started. I eventually became discouraged every time I would look at my own blog, and slowly but surely I became critical of the very thing I had once been excited about. My enthusiasm flickered like a candlewick struggling to stay lit in a windstorm. I even caught myself saying things like:

- "I will never be as good as them."
- "I might as well just focus on something else."
- "Why am I kidding myself? No one will want to read my stuff."
- "You're not an author. You're just trying to force something to happen."

I definitely became my own worst critic in every shape, fashion, and form. Before long I didn't feel like blogging at all. My creativity crashed, and I couldn't regain focus no matter what I did. Dreams of writing a book became an idea that seemed impossible to attain. This caused my emotions to go all out of control. One day I would sit at my computer energized and ready to push out a great blog post, only to be overcome by a feeling of failure because I had looked at someone's website before I started. I would get nauseous at the very thought of writing. Trust me—that's not a good place to be.

In the midst of a depressing moment one day while I sat staring at my computer trying to write, a thought broke through the darkness and brought a light of revelation. I realized that comparing myself to others was only slowing me down from doing what I was called to do. I realized that I wasn't called to be like anyone else. I was called to be me, and I could be me better than anyone else in the world—years of experience or not! I realized that if I had a desire to write, then it must be for a reason, and maybe that reason was to encourage and inspire others into action and reaching their Next. Over the next few weeks, I became overwhelmingly comfortable at just being me and I regained my passion for writing.

> Today you are you, that is truer than true.
> There is no one alive who is youer than you. —Dr. Seuss

Just like I'm the best at being me, you're the best at being you!

I want you to write out a few examples of how you have compared yourself with others. This is not to point out your faults but to identify the distraction of comparison in your life so you can quickly recognize it on your journey and avoid it instantly. Remember, you can be you better than anyone else!

Ways I've compared myself with others:

1.

2.

3.

It's also just as important to know what unique qualities you have. Knowing your uniqueness can serve as guardrails that will keep you from crossing over into the lane of comparing yourself with others. It also helps you to remain true to the person you are.

Take a moment to write down a few qualities that are dominant in your life:

My unique qualities:

1.

2.

3.

4. The Distraction of People

Let's face it—there are some people who are not called to go where you are going. If they are not going with you, then by all means don't let them keep you from your destiny. Not everyone you share your dream with will be supportive. In fact, some people will be the voice of negativity and will suck the passion right out of you if you let them. They may tell you things like, "That's impossible," or "I tried that and it never worked." You must understand that their skepticism could very well be a result of their life being stuck in a rut. Regardless of the naysayers, you must keep moving forward.

Usually when you share your 10x20 dream with someone who has a 3x5 dream, the conversation goes opposite of how you thought it would go. The other person is neither excited about your dream nor supportive of you going after it. It's not that they don't believe in you; it's just that your dream probably exceeds their imagination and they don't even believe it's possible.

As you continue to move forward, some of your friends or family members may become jealous of your newfound desire and passion to excel and do more with your life. If a friend or family member is overcome with the green-eyed monster and begins to show resentment toward you, that's when you have to realize that people are human, especially your family members and friends.

Don't take it personally or feel threatened. And by all means don't let the fear of losing a close relationship stop you from reaching your dream.

They may feel jealous because they see you doing what they have been too scared to do all their life. Still, don't let this cause you to divert your focus. Stay the course, and sooner or later they will realize that they can go after their dreams as well. You just might be the trailblazer they need to get them from where they are in life to where they desire to be!

5. The Distraction of Regret

The distraction of regret has imprisoned many people along their journey—and it is always a self-imposed sentence. The prison of regret is a place in which the prisoner is his or her own warden. But there's no reason to stay stuck in yesterday or in what could have been. Just because you miss one opportunity doesn't mean that another opportunity won't ever come around. If you focus on yesterday's loss, you will never see tomorrow's door of opportunity!

> Take responsibility for where you are.
> Take action for where you want to be.

If you've ever lived with small children, at one time or another your television entertainment consisted of Walt Disney movies. The story of one certain movie, *Planes*, really caught my attention.

A crop-duster plane named Dusty had a dream of becoming something more than what he was created for. He wanted to race other planes. He met an older plane named Skipper, a seasoned naval aviator, who became his mentor. Skipper told Dusty exciting stories about all the wars that he had flown in and all the missions he got to be part of. However, we find out that Skipper has a fear of flying and the reason for his fear is revealed when he tells Dusty about something that happened in his past.

One day when Skipper was leading young new recruit planes back to the base, they wanted to dive below the clouds and Skipper told them no. But they kept asking until he finally gave in and led them on a dive below the clouds. What they couldn't see were the enemy ships in the waters below, and they flew right into an ambush. That horrible day Skipper witnessed all of those young planes fall to their end. The regret kept him grounded for years.

This simple story might remind you of some event in your past that has kept you in a prison of regret. Maybe you made a mistake years ago and you can't get past it. Or maybe you experienced a divorce or failure and you've been blaming yourself for years, unable to move on—even if everyone else involved has forgiven and forgotten.

You will never get to your Next if you don't free yourself from the prison of regret. Maybe you need to forgive yourself. Or you might need to forgive others. Whatever it is, just do it. You have no idea how many lives you will greatly impact by reaching your Next—you simply can't afford to stay tangled up in regret!

Back to the Disney story: Dusty is about to race in the Grand Race of all planes. That same day Skipper, the older fearful plane, overhears a conversation between a gang of planes that are planning to take Dusty out of commission in a part of the course that is surrounded by mountains. Skipper is then faced with a big decision! He can either stay in the prison of regret or he can free himself and help Dusty reach his dreams.

I'm glad to report that he chose the latter of the two. He got past his regret and took to the skies for the first time in years. He also reached Dusty just in time to help him reach his dreams.

It all comes down to your decision to free yourself from regret. If you find yourself stuck in the past, my hope is that you will find the strength and determination to propel yourself beyond those prison bars. Just believe there is something more waiting for you. Move past the pain of yesterday and into the freedom of today.

It's time for you to fly again, my friend.

6. The Distraction of Failure

We are hindered by past disappointments and hurts. The very thought of failing again seems unbearable at times. You might become paralyzed in your progress if you are not completely over a past hurt.

Failure has also developed such a bad stigma. Nobody wants to fail at anything for fear of how they might look to others.

We can get so consumed meditating on our disappointments that we are totally drained of the energy needed to get back up and try again. Fear of ending up in the same boat filled with pain, hurt, and regret is the very thing that keeps you standing on the shore instead of getting back in the water and trying again. News flash: just because you failed at something doesn't make you a failure.

> Every strike brings me closer to the next home run.
> —Babe Ruth

Have you ever heard of a man by the name of Milton Hershey? Of course you have. He is the creator of Hershey's Chocolate. I'm sure you've had one of his candy bars or the famous Hershey's Kisses before. You know his chocolate is delicious, but what you might not know is that Milton Hershey had two failed businesses before he got on the right track of successfully coming up with the milk chocolate treat that millions of people enjoy today.

He wasn't distracted by his failures. With each failure came more wisdom and knowledge for his next attempt. His perseverance finally paid off, and now the world indulges in the fruit of his labor—or should I say the chocolate of his labor.

So get up, dust yourself off, and keep moving forward. Every successful person is acquainted with failure. The difference is that their failures never distracted them from reaching their dreams.

> I didn't fail, I just found 2,000 ways not to
> make a light bulb. —Thomas Edison

Don't let a temporary failure stop you from creating a permanent success. You must keep pushing no matter what. Failures have the ability serve as great teachers along the journey, but we must quit looking at failure as having the last word. It's time to change your perspective and let your failures teach you to be wiser and smarter, because there is a future beyond your failures.

7. The Distraction of Perfectionism

If you're waiting to be perfect at something before starting, then you will probably never start. Just do it and learn perfection along the way.

When we are overly concerned about not being perfect, we stay in planning mode forever, hesitant to step out and try something new. We buy into the lie that says, "If you can't do it perfectly, then don't do it at all." Don't be distracted by this frustrating killer of dreams. Here's a revelation for you: you are not perfect and you never will be perfect—and that's perfectly okay!—so don't worry yourself to death by trying to reach an unattainable goal.

8. The Paralysis of Perfectionism

This is such a big distraction that it warrants a little more discussion. Perfectionism is defined as the tendency to set unrealistically high standards for performance of oneself and others, along with the inability to accept mistakes. But wanting to be perfect at something you've never done before is expecting way too much of yourself. The antidote for the paralysis of perfectionism is action—any action at all!

> Anything worth doing is worth doing poorly—
> until you can learn to do it well. —Zig Ziglar

In a leadership culture, we are taught to do things with excellence. I believe in that and continue to practice it. The harsh reality is no one ever does anything for the first time with excellence. A perfect performance is actually the result of imperfect practice. Excellence is acquired through a series of events called *trial, error,* and *repeat until done right.* Don't let perfectionism paralyze you from taking the next step you need to march your way into greatness.

A perfectionist usually doesn't want to do anything unless they can do it perfectly and with excellence. While they're on the sidelines thinking, calculating, planning, and waiting to do it perfectly, others are already on the field learning from experience.

I think that perfectionism has a lot to do with self-image. Many people strive to be perfect or do things perfectly because they fear what others will think if they don't. They become consumed with projecting a perfect image for others to see, and that becomes an unhealthy driving force in all their endeavors.

> Waiting to do something perfectly only prohibits you from practicing that which you may be destined to do excellently one day.

If you are ever going to move forward into your Next, you will have to let go of any perfectionist mentality that may be in the back of your mind. Just start where you are. When you're stepping out of your comfort zone and trying to do the next new thing, you probably won't do it right the first time. Chances are you won't do it right the second, third, fourth, fifth, or even sixth time! But that's okay. You will get better the more you keep practicing.

Take a deep breath. Embrace trial and error, and eventually you'll find yourself doing it with excellence.

> Get a good idea, and stay with it. Dog it, and work at it until it's done, and done right. —Walt Disney

Even Walt Disney knew the power of starting with imperfection and working your way up. That's a great way of utilizing time, and it gets you moving in the right direction. While others are still in the boardroom meeting and planning, you will be on the road to your destination.

Done with Distractions

If you have been plagued with distractions, here is a simple tip that can help keep you focused. Tape a few motivating quotes on your bathroom mirror. Yes, you have to actually do it. It doesn't count if you just look them up online and bookmark them on your computer. Actually write them out on a piece of paper and tape it to your mirror or wall where you will see it every day.

The goal is to stare at the quotes at least once a day and get them so ingrained in your mind that you will find yourself thinking about them throughout the day. These will keep you focused on the task at hand and help guard against the awful energy drain of distraction. I sometimes take it a step further and actually write out some quotes or even some of my favorite Bible verses on several 3x5 note cards and carry them around with me for easy access, especially when I can anticipate a potentially challenging day.

Chapter 5

THE SEDUCTION OF
SETTLEVILLE

Sometimes people with big dreams, plans, potential, and ideas end up settling for less than they deserve or desire. For one reason or another, they never take that leap of faith that had the potential to launch them into their destiny. Maybe life circumstances, regrets, and disappointments left them with a feeling of hopelessness, so they settle into a life that is less fulfilling than the one they dreamed about.

Settleville is a stagnant place, a passion killer, and a dream stealer. When people buy into the lie that they can never have more or that their time for greatness has passed, they settle into their frustrations and accept an unfulfilling life. Some people even try to convince themselves that this is the best they can do. They force themselves to become happy where they are, but I wonder if they are truly happy at all.

> A happy man is too satisfied with the present to dwell
> too much on the future. —Albert Einstein

It is fairly easy to move into Settleville but much harder to leave because it quickly becomes familiar, and we love familiarity. We like knowing what our days and weeks will look like. Many people will come to Settleville and pitch their tent and make the most out of a mediocre situation. While it's good to be thankful for what you do have, if a feeling of familiarity keeps you from taking a step forward in order to accomplish greatness, then familiarity needs to be kicked to the curb! Once you buy into the lie that you can't—or shouldn't—have more, your mind immediately tries to find happiness with a life that is less than you imagined. This coping mechanism starts working overtime until your dream is a distant memory.

When you let go of your big dreams and exchange them for a place of comfort, ease, and having just enough, your discarded dream becomes a black hole that eventually sucks the life right out of you.

We can all agree that this scenario sounds miserable. No one wants to live a mediocre life; no one wants to look twenty or thirty years down the road and see that nothing has changed. But it happens all the time—to well-meaning, big-dreaming people.

The question is, why does this happen so often? And how can we prevent the permanent move to Settleville?

John Maxwell wrote an article in which he stated several reasons why dreams never take flight.* I immediately saw two reasons why the move to Settleville happens so often:

1. We fall into the habit of settling for average.

Humans are movers and doers by nature. But we're also quick to stop when we encounter roadblocks. In a culture that surrounds

---

* The points are written by John Maxwell but I expound on each one myself. John Maxwell, "5 Reasons Why Dreams Don't Take Flight," *Success*, October 21, 2014, http://www.success.com/article/john-c-maxwell-5-reasons-why-dreams-dont -take-flight.

us with options for every scenario imaginable, sometimes we become overwhelmed when we need to mentally dig in and overcome instead.

We're bound to stumble upon obstacles, unforeseen circumstances, or tough decisions along the way. But it's become easier for some to give in and to make no attempt to get through it than to fight back and move forward. While the effort required to break through could be quite small, our minds tell us that it's too much trouble or that it will require far too much emotional and physical energy to press through and continue. In an effort to clear our conscious of the act of settling, we convince ourselves that what we have now is good enough—at least it's more than what we used to have. So we often settle for average when greatness may be only a few steps away.

2. We lack the confidence needed to pursue our dreams.

Many people lack confidence. While they may find it easy to see the confidence in others, for some reason, they fall short when it comes to acknowledging the value that they possess deep down inside. Also, people often see fear as a sign of lacking confidence, and that couldn't be further from the truth. Just because fear is present doesn't mean that confidence is not. Fear is only an obstacle along the way to your destiny. Confidence will help you overcome it.

Then there's the past, the old skeletons in the closet, the play-by-play of every mistake you've ever made. Some people allow their past failures and mistakes to haunt them and seduce them into the dark corners of Settleville. They don't want the embarrassment of failure again, or they simply don't want to be hurt or disappointed if they never achieve success.

I'm convinced that if Settleville were a physical town, the following types of "future" people would populate it:

- CEOs of great companies
- Innovators with the next breakthrough in technology
- Doctors who were destined to save thousands of lives
- Congressmen and congresswomen who would change the nation
- Professional athletes who would serve as great role models
- Teachers who would shape the mind of the next Albert Einstein

What powerful impact could you have on the future if you can avoid Settleville?

Now, this is where you have to be honest with yourself. You know whether or not you are settling for something less than what you could be doing with your life. It's one thing to be stuck in Settleville and not know you're there. This would mean you are clueless to the fact that there is more for your life than what you are experiencing now. It's another thing to be in Settleville and *know* you are there. You have that gut feeling that there is more in life for you.

If you know you're in Settleville, you have a decision to make. You can stay stuck, or you can pack your bags and get ready to move out! If you're ready to pack your bags, congratulations! Now you'll need to concentrate on your next steps to ensure you have the best plan of action:

1. Make a list of the area(s) in your life where you feel like you have settled.

2. Once that list is compiled, come up with two to three action steps that will cause you to gain some momentum and get you moving in the right direction.

   For example, let's say you're working at a dead-end job that pays minimum wage with no hint of a raise or advancement in sight. Your next step would be to write out two to three things you can do *right now* that will eventually open up a door for you to step into something much better. You don't have to quit your job. But you can begin to make changes that will allow you to quit your job in time. These could include going back to school to further your education or taking online courses that are geared toward a new career you are interested in. Action steps might also include pulling together a resume and submitting it to other places of employment.

3. Schedule at least one activity for sometime this week—even today if you can. Don't put your progress off until next week. The sooner you take the first step, the better.

PART II

SO WHAT'S NEXT?

Sometimes trying to figure out where to go from here can be the hardest part about your journey. Moving from where you are to where you want to be will always require taking the necessary steps to clear a pathway to your goal. They don't have to be big giant steps all at once, but they should challenge you to make some pretty important decisions so you can steer your life in the direction of your dreams.

Chapter 6

WHEN YOU KNOW THERE'S SOMETHING MORE

O n my life's journey, I always knew when a shift was coming because I had an uneasy feeling that change was about to happen. I'd be happy where I was for a period of time, but then a feeling of discontentment would start to settle in. Things that I used to be passionate about would all of a sudden no longer give me fulfillment. Slowly but surely I would reach a place where I would have to give myself a pep talk before I even went to work. You've probably been there too.

Looking Back and Moving Forward

With a career of more than twenty years in full-time ministry, I can look back and see how each step led to the next and how all the puzzle pieces fit together to get me to where I am today. But while I was in the middle of it, I didn't always see how my next step would make an impact. Sometimes I didn't even know what my next step was!

Back in 1990, I had just graduated from Roosevelt High School in San Antonio, Texas, and was clueless about my future. After my parents' rough divorce left us depleted in every way, my mother, sister, and I ended up living in one bedroom of my aunt's two-bedroom apartment. Plans and dreams I'd had for college dwindled and turned into a big, blank unknown. Instead of getting ready for college, I took a volunteer position as an activities director in a nursing home facility that was within walking distance of the apartment. I really enjoyed working with the elderly. From hosting bingo time, to making donuts, to speaking at the residents' weekly church services there, I gave that job my all, and it was evident to the staff. I was eventually hired for a full-time position and was very happy in my role.

At that time, I was also active at my church as a youth leader. My youth pastor, Bill, was my first mentor. Little by little he would give me responsibility in the youth ministry, which eventually led to me feeling a call to the ministry. I still remember the first time he gave me the keys to the church building. An event was running late and he asked me to stay and lock the building. A youth leader with keys to the building—could there be anything better? Wow, I thought I had just arrived.

However, after a few years of being there at the church and working at the nursing home, I began to feel that something was missing. I couldn't put my finger on it at first. Yes, I was thankful for my opportunities and grateful for my job and my mentor, but I knew there was a next step for me somewhere else. Shortly after that I began to feel a strong desire to attend a Bible college in Columbus, Texas, which was about two and a half hours away.

By that time things had changed at home, and my sister, Jackie, and I were sharing a one-bedroom apartment and a car. Yet I still kept feeling the desire to leave and attend Bible college.

I finally called the school to inquire about classes, only to hear that the semester had already started and that I should wait until the following year. Although I was disappointed, I quickly realized it would give me enough time to save money for tuition and my sister time to get a roommate and purchase a vehicle as well.

Sometimes your Next is not now.
Timing is everything.

When I arrived at Bible college the next year, it was the first time I felt like I was really on my own—away from family, friends, and the rest of the world. I mean that literally because this Bible college was located on 553 acres in the middle of nowhere. I remember thinking to myself one day as I sat outside my dorm, "What in the world am I doing here?" When we take a step of faith in a direction we believe is correct, sometimes it doesn't quite look or feel like we thought it would. That doesn't mean that we made a mistake. It simply means that every step doesn't have to make us feel good in the beginning. Needless to say, my time in Bible college laid the foundation for my life's calling of ministry and serving others.

While in Bible school, I had the opportunity to be one of the assistants to the school president. Many of the other students would have loved to have my job. The president would often be invited to speak at different churches and functions, and as his assistant, I would go along, often traveling all over the world. I thought I would keep that position forever because I loved it so much! But after two years, the uneasiness began to creep in.

After a while I started feeling like I was supposed to be doing more with my life at this stage, though I couldn't explain it. So I told myself, "This is the best job I've ever had. I'm traveling the world and having a blast!" I tried to push past the feeling of discontentment, but I couldn't. I ignored it for a while, but my happiness in my job began to slip away day by day.

My feeling of unhappiness wasn't caused by the place where I was working. In fact, it was a very successful Bible school and ministry with a great staff of people, and it continues to reach hundreds of thousands of people to this day. So it wasn't the work environment that was causing me to be unhappy; it was the fact that I knew there was more for me to do. The more I ignored it, the more the feeling of discontentment would overwhelm me. It was then that I knew I had to take a step toward my Next.

So after completing the Bible school program and working there for nearly three years, I informed them that I would be leaving. Everyone was supportive even though they were sad to see me go. The next step in my journey was a job as a children's pastor in my hometown of San Antonio, Texas. And years later, that job led me to Nashville—where I've grown career wise, where I met my wife, and where we are raising our family.

Every next step you take is all a part of your journey. I'm so glad I decided to take that first leap of faith—moving away from home to attend Bible college—that would ultimately serve as a catalyst to start my new journey. It was scary, but I did it anyway. I was alone, but I did it anyway. No matter your circumstances, you can do it anyway too! If you have a feeling that there's something more for your life, you will have to take the leap of faith sooner or later if you ever want to reach your full potential and live the life you're dreaming about.

Maybe you are at the crossroads right now. Deep down inside there's a feeling telling you that there is more out there for you. You are excited, anxious, and nervous all at the same time. You've been dealing with the emotions of discontentment and unhappiness in your current situation, and it's draining you every day just to keep going. If this sounds familiar, know that change is coming.

> Being discontent is not being ungrateful.
> Sometimes you just know there's something more for you.

Taking Great Leaps of Faith

All great leaders have taken the leap at one time or another. Sooner or later you will also have to take a leap of faith either in your life, job, career, or family. The leap of faith doesn't necessarily make things easier, but it does make your future possible. You will have to do something that comes with a great risk while carrying a great reward. You might have to let go of your *now* in order to seize your *Next*.

Feeling overwhelmed? Just look at some of the leaps of faith others have made, with great results:

- Apple CEO, Steve Jobs, took a leap and changed the world with technology.
- Henry Ford took a leap, and now we are all getting around a little faster.
- Sidney Poitier took a leap and broke the race barrier in American cinema.

You may not be able to see the big picture just yet, but when you know there's something more, you can start forming a mental picture in your mind of the possibilities that may lie ahead. Allow yourself to dream of your future!

Helpful Tip

It's always important to be fully aware of each risk involved in your endeavors. It's equally as important to be fully aware of the potential rewards. Take some time to write out the risk and reward for some of your upcoming endeavors.

Endeavor 1:

Risk:

Reward:

Endeavor 2:

Risk:

Reward:

Endeavor 3:

Risk:

Reward:

Chapter 7

GETTING UNSTUCK

Whether you're stuck in a job, situation, or circumstance, the feeling of going nowhere is simply no fun at all. It's time to get you moving back in the direction of your dreams. You can do it. All you need is a little push.

> Being stuck is a choice. If you're there,
> just know that you don't have to stay there.

Remember how I mentioned that my Bible school was out in the middle of nowhere? Since it was in the country there were a lot of dirt roads. One day I was out on detail, driving through the property in a small pickup truck to check on students and staff after the rainstorm. I decided to drive by one of the dorms that was located off the side of a hill. Everything in me was telling me that the road was too wet and that I would probably get stuck if I tried to go that route. Well, I did it anyway, and guess what? I got stuck.

There I was, grinding gears, riding the clutch, and trying to gain some traction, but nothing was working. The tires were just spinning around, throwing mud all over the side of the dorm as

GETTING UNSTUCK • 67

the truck continued to sink deeper and deeper into a rut. I soon realized I couldn't get the truck out on my own. I needed help. Fortunately some other staff members came to my rescue. The first thing one of them said was, "This has happened to me many times, so don't worry, we will get you out." He gave me instructions, and the others pushed and rocked the truck back and forth. He told me when to shift gears and how much to accelerate. In just a few short minutes, the truck was out and I was no longer stuck.

The truth is that we have all been in a similar situation at one time or another—we are stuck and unable to continue on the same path. We get irritated and aggravated at the littlest thing. We also tend to blame others for our lack of forward progress. It's in those moments that you must learn to control your emotions by ignoring the voices of the Mind Monsters that are trying to trip you up. It also helps to be aware of the signs of being stuck so you can navigate yourself away from the situation as soon as possible.

Warning Signs of Being Stuck

Anger

Any little thing can set you off in the worst way. When you blow your cool, it's not pretty.

Irritation

Things that didn't bother you at all in the past now all of a sudden are like sandpaper to your skin. Your tolerance for people is very low, and you find it difficult to enjoy the simple things in life.

Sense of Hopelessness

You may find yourself coming home at the end of the day and wanting to just be by yourself. You don't want to have any family time because you are exhausted. You go into a room by yourself and isolate because nobody understands what you are going through. This never turns out well and has the potential to cause you to sink into a deep, dark hole of depression.

Jealousy

Deep down inside, you start resenting others when good things happen for them. What's worse is when a close friend or family member reaches success and you find it difficult to celebrate with them. You now despise the success of the very people that you should be happy for.

My wife and I had to learn how to conquer jealousy when we were trying to get pregnant with our first child. We already knew in advance that it wasn't going to be easy for us to get pregnant. The doctor told my wife at an early age that she would probably never have kids. We tried for nearly a year without getting pregnant.

All of a sudden everyone around us was getting pregnant. Every time we turned around, another friend or neighbor was expecting! Our emotions were on a roller-coaster ride as we fought the feelings of jealousy while still trying to be genuinely happy and excited for others around us. We chose to be happy for them while still contending with the disappointment that we were currently experiencing in our lives. It wasn't easy, but we pushed through and we did it.

We eventually got pregnant—twice—and have two beautiful children.

Unstick Yourself

One young man I mentored found himself stuck in life. By the time he reached out to me, he had already started taking the

GETTING UNSTUCK · 69

necessary steps to point his life back in the right direction; he was just looking for a little guidance to help keep him going and on the right track. He was in his midtwenties and basically going nowhere really fast. He'd surrounded himself with friends who where in the same boat, and they were all traveling to Settleville together. He was a single father of three beautiful children but was living a life far below his potential, and he knew it.

When I asked him what caused him to turn his life around, his answer was powerful. He said, "I took a hard look at my life and was honest with myself. I have three children, had no job, and was basically couch surfing from house to house with my friends. I told myself that this lifestyle can't go on. I knew there was something more in me than what I was doing. I knew I needed to change."

And that's exactly what he did. He made a drastic change and started making better choices and decisions. He got a job and became more productive with his life. He started surrounding himself with friendships that had positive influences on his life, since he knew that if he wanted to get unstuck he couldn't hang out with people who were stuck themselves. He got his life back on track, and it all started because he made a decision to not stay stuck.

And now it's your turn to unstick yourself. You may be …

- … stuck in a dead-end job.
- … stuck in a relationship that is unfulfilling.
- … stuck in a city or town that you have lived in all of your life.
- … stuck in a position in a company and don't see a chance of promotion.
- … stuck because you don't have a better education.

> ... stuck because you don't have enough money in the bank.
> ... stuck in a mind-set that you can never have more or be more.

No matter what your situation is, the good news is you can change it by making a decision to get yourself unstuck and moving again. Remember, you have the power to change your thinking, which will ultimately change your life. Don't settle for less than when you are destined for greatness. Take control of your destiny and start reaching for the life that you have imagined.

Next Steps to Getting Unstuck

By now you've identified at least one area in life where you feel stuck, and that's great! Knowing what you need to improve on is always the first step to getting to where you want to be.

We also learned to identify the early warning signs that tend to indicate the presence of a Mind Monster or a distraction in your way. When you feel your thoughts heading in a wrong direction, it's important that you stop right then and there and address that particular feeling or emotion. Let the Mind Monster know that you are not going to allow your thoughts to go in that direction. It might even require you to speak to your own mind in some cases:

- "I will not be jealous of others."
- "I am not going to let this frustration get the best of me."
- "I am moving forward to my Next."
- "My best days are ahead of me."

Do whatever you have to do to get your mind moving in a positive direction once again. Begin to focus on what you want your future to look like—imagine every detail! Visualize yourself accomplishing your dream. By doing this, it puts your mind on a different thought track, and you will end up in a much better place emotionally.

Pretty soon you'll find yourself unstuck and gaining momentum toward your goal. What are you waiting for? It's time to get moving!

Chapter 8

QUIT BELIEVING
THE LIES

Another important key to getting unstuck and moving forward is learning to stop believing the lies that bombard your mind from time to time. What you believe has the potential to move you into your dreams or stop you from ever trying to reach something that you are passionate about.

People will often sit and entertain those little lies that run through their minds until they actually believe them. I even know a few people who have been told all of their lives by relatives that they were no good and that they would never amount to anything. Sadly, they grew up believing those painful, hurtful words and never even dreamed of doing anything more with their lives. They bought into the lie for many years, and it cost them their dreams and fulfillment. It wasn't until they finally stopped believing the lies that they could dream and reach for more.

I had to quit believing a few key things in order to go after my dreams. Chances are you may believe some of the same lies I once believed.

It's too late to be successful.

If you continue to believe that it's too late for you, then you will never develop enough enthusiasm to even begin the endeavor. It's *not* too late for you. Start now. Take action now. Get up and get going in the direction of your dreams, and get ready for the ride of a lifetime.

> Whether you think you can,
> or you think you can't—you're right. —Henry Ford

Success is only for others.

Sometimes it's easy to get caught up in the success of others. When this happens, you usually compare your worst to their best instead of comparing where you were to where you are today. Success is for anyone who will do what it takes to make it happen. The truth is that you can be successful if you set your mind to it and believe that you can. And stop comparing yourself to other people!

Success will happen on its own.

Success at anything takes work, work, and more work. Nothing will happen if you just sit around all day waiting for good fortune to fall into your lap. A good friend of mine says that being a success means you have to get out there and hustle every day. That's right, every day you have to make the connections, do the tasks, attack your to-do list, stay focused, and follow through, just to wake up and do it all over again the next day. But hard work pays off in the end. Go ahead and roll up those sleeves and get after it.

> It is good to dream, but it is better to dream and work. Faith
> is mighty, but action with faith is mightier.
> Desiring is helpful, but work and desire are invincible.
> —Thomas Robert Gaines

You can't.

Take the words *I can't* out of your everyday vocabulary. I'm a firm believer that if you have a passionate dream about doing something, then that's an indicator that you are qualified to take the first step in that direction. You may not have the total ability just yet to accomplish the goal, but you do have the ability to get started in the right direction. Take the first step, keep walking, and the rest will come. Quit believing *you can't* and start believing *you can.*

Your past failures can stop your future.

This is a pretty big one here. If you're like me, then there are probably some things in your past that you're not too proud of—things that you hope no one ever finds out.

I used to believe I had made too many mistakes and that those mistakes would mean I wouldn't be able to fulfill my purpose in life. I battled with those thoughts for years until I finally made the decision to put the past where it belonged—in my past!

Your past is behind you for a reason; that's why it's called your past. Quit looking back and start looking forward. Some people spend so much emotional energy trying to change things that have happened in their past. If you're one of these people, let me free you of this: no amount of emotional energy can ever change what happened in your past. Instead of being threatened by your past, decide to let your past be your present educator. Learn from it and become wiser in your endeavor to reach your dreams. Quit believing this major lie, hold your head up high, and get ready for the next thing in your life. There is a future beyond your failures. Whatever you do, keep looking forward.

If you are ever going to get unstuck and get on with your life, you will have to stop believing these lies once and for all. Stop buying into them and your world will change. Once you do this, it will create momentum and energy within you to go after your Next without hesitation.

For now, let's identify any lies you have believed about yourself that are still holding you back from your dreams.

Lies I need to stop believing:

Chapter 9

LETTING GO OF YESTERDAY

W e just talked about letting go of past failures. But we also need to talk about letting go of past comforts. You can't go after the next new thing while still trying to hold on to the old thing—no matter how good it feels. Change can be good. It can propel you forward.

When we signed our four-year-old son up for T-ball, I started practicing with him. We spent time in the backyard, practicing hitting the ball and grounding fielders. I taught him how to hit with a Nerf baseball bat and plastic Wiffle balls. But a couple of weeks before his first T-ball practice with his team, I bought him a real bat and ball because I knew they would be using the real thing for T-ball.

When I brought the new bat and ball home, he was excited (just like I thought he would be), but he also looked at me and said, "What about my other bat?" I quickly said, "This is your new bat for T-ball."

When we practiced with it for the first time, he took a couple of swings and then began to whine for his old bat. He said the new bat was too heavy, he couldn't hit with it, and he wanted his old one back because it was better.

At that point I was a little frustrated because he was arguing with me instead of understanding that I was trying to help him. And that little aluminum bat wasn't cheap!

I knew I was going to have to change his mind-set quickly and that I had to communicate on a level that he could understand. I told him that the Nerf bat was for when he was younger, like his little sister, and that now he was a big boy about to play T-ball, and that was for big boys. He then said, "Oh, the Nerf bat is for babies and I'm not a baby anymore, Daddy. I'm a big boy." He got it! And pretty soon he was able to swing the new bat just as well as the old one. It just took letting go of what was comfortable.

When something new is happening in your life, sometimes the struggle you encounter is the very act of letting go of the old thing. The feeling of familiarity and comfort can keep you from taking the steps you need to take to be effective in your next season.

My encouragement for you today is to let go of:

- old mind-sets that are enslaving you;
- old routines that are boring you;
- old ways of thinking that are slowing your progress;
- old expectations that are disappointing you;
- old associations that are draining you; and
- old habits that are hindering you.

> If you bring your yesterday into your tomorrow,
> then your future will always be the same.

Let go of past successes and past failures. Make room for the new thing that is coming your way. Be willing, ready, and able to step away from your comfort zone; let go of the things that have become too familiar. Don't be afraid to venture out into unfamiliar territory. Your greatest accomplishment just might be the one you never thought you would be able to do!

Let Go of What Didn't Happen

We've all had those times in our lives when we were expecting something to happen and it didn't, only to leave us disappointed.

- You thought the relationship would work out and it didn't.
- You thought you were next in line for the promotion, and to your surprise, it went to someone else.
- You put your trust in someone and they let you down.
- You thought a door of opportunity was opening for you, and then all of a sudden, for reasons out of your control, it closed.

Your reaction to a closed door of opportunity can either propel you into your future or enslave you in your present. But if you stand there trying to figure out the why, you will never see your Next.

> You have to learn to let go of what *didn't* happen
> so you can get ready to experience what *can* happen.

When a door closes, quit standing there looking at it. This is not the end of the world, no matter how you feel about it. How you respond is the key to overcoming this moment. If a door suddenly closes, you're now in a good position to turn around and start looking for the next opportunity coming your way. Keep your head up and your emotions in check. Don't start blaming others for the closed opportunity—blame shifting will keep you stuck. And quit trying to figure out all the reasons why it didn't happen. Relax! You are right where you are supposed to be. A closed door can lead to a great opportunity. Keep moving. Keep dreaming. Keep reaching. Whatever you do, don't stop.

The answer to your why will come—maybe even around the time you walk through the next open door of opportunity. Then you will be able to see why the other door closed. It had to close. It needed to close. It was supposed to close so you could enjoy the rewards of the next opportunity. So the next time you encounter a closed door, quickly move on and expect that something greater is about to happen for you.

Several years ago, before I moved to Nashville, I was in a transitional period, in between jobs, and searching for the next big thing to do with my life. I had been an associate pastor, speaker, and communicator for several years and felt like somehow that was going to go to another level.

I met a gentleman through a close friend of mine, and he was impressed with my speaking ability. He said that if I gave him a few of my recorded messages, he would pass them along to his connections and have me speaking all over the place. This was the big door of opportunity I'd been waiting for! But like many of us often do, I put all my trust and hope in one person. After I gave him my material, I didn't hear back from him.

Several years later I ran into him at a conference. We greeted one another, and I introduced him to my wife, Heather. After a brief conversation we went our separate ways. I realized then that if he had opened doors for me years before, like he said he would, I may have never moved to Nashville where I met my amazing wife. The disappointment I'd felt back then didn't compare to the overwhelming joy I was experiencing in my present stage of life. That day I got a great reminder that everything happens—or doesn't happen—for a reason.

Forgive the Past Hurts and Move Forward

We have all been wronged, betrayed, or taken advantage of at least a time or two. We may have memories of a painful experience or event with another person that still bother us today. Whether you've been hurt by a family member, friend, coworker, or a spouse, it's time to forgive and let it go.

Unforgiveness has the power to keep us from moving forward while the person we are angry with has moved on with his or her life. While they are free, we are held captive by memories and emotions that continue to drain us of energy and ambition.

> Unforgiveness is like holding a hot coal in your hand
> and being mad at the person who started the fire.
> Forgive, drop it, and let it go.

If you're ready to stop the pain and let go of the past and forgive, here are a few suggestions and examples for you to consider of simple steps to take toward walking in freedom from the past.

Three Simple Steps Toward Forgiveness

1) Acknowledge the unforgiveness.

It doesn't do you any good to ignore the emotions of bitterness or even anger that you have toward another person for what they did to you. The sooner you acknowledge the fact that you are holding a grudge, the sooner you can devise a plan to be free of it once and for all.

2) Write a letter to the person you need to forgive.

It may take you several tries or revisions before you are happy with your results, but it isn't just for them; this is an activity that will help you release hard feelings. Most people are better at communicating when they write it out first. Put lots of thought into it, as this is an important key to forgiving and moving forward. Trust me, you will begin to feel the forgiveness as you see the words that you are writing in the letter. And make sure to include the words *I forgive you.*

3) Make a plan to contact that person.

For some it may be a phone conversation. For others it may be an email or a face-to-face conversation. If all else fails, send the letter you wrote with your own handwriting. They may have forgotten about it or may not even know that you are carrying unforgiveness toward them. Whatever the case is, it's important for you to follow through and communicate to that person that you are forgiving them.

If the person is no longer living, it is still important to write the letter—for your own sake. You can then decide to throw it away, burn it, tear it up, or otherwise discard it. It can also help to visit a gravestone or any location that either reminds you of that person or brings you peace. Then, even if you feel a little uncertain about having a conversation with yourself, speak your thoughts out loud as though that person were listening. Just the action of getting the thoughts out of your mind and into the air can be very freeing.

Now, as a word of precaution, this step doesn't apply to everyone. There may be some situations in which it is not healthy or advisable to reopen communication between you and the person that caused the offense. Know that personal contact is not necessary in order to forgive and move on.

Next Steps

This part may require a little soul searching, but it's definitely worth it.

Take some time when you can be alone and uninterrupted and look back over your life. Try to pinpoint any negative experiences from your past that you have carried over into your present. This is not to get you to relive a painful part of your past, but it will allow you to identify those negative things you are still holding on to.

Once they are identified, you have to make a conscious decision to let them go and move on. It doesn't mean that the hurt or disappointment will go away immediately, but it does mean that it will go away eventually as you commit—and continue to recommit—to your decision of letting it go. Forgiveness is often a process, so don't feel like you have to grant forgiveness once and then never think about the past offense again. You may have to forgive the offense several times, or at least as often as it comes into your thoughts and bothers you.

Another good thing to do is talk to someone about it. Holding in hurts or disappointments only allows them to continue to grow and worsen over a period of time. Reach out to someone you can trust and talk about it with them. Sometimes we just need to get things off our chest before we can let it go and move on.

Chapter 10

START DREAMING AGAIN

The beginning stages of reaching your future will require that you dream and visualize your ideal future. A dream has the power and potential to encourage, motivate, and excite you in the early stages of the process.

It's very important to write down your dreams and goals while they are fresh and unchallenged. I actually have a notebook that I use to keep track of my thoughts and ideas. It also helps me stay accountable to my vision.

Remember that when you start moving in the direction of your dream, you will no doubt be met with challenges and discouraging moments. Not everyone will jump on your bandwagon and sing your praises. You will take a few rides on the emotional roller coaster. However, in those moments when you begin to doubt yourself, if you've written down your dreams and goals, you will be able to read your initial thoughts from when you were bursting with excitement. This will help you regain your focus and bring stability to wavering emotions. Your dreams are as tangible as you make them. If it's written down, then it can be rehearsed, revisited, and remembered.

Believe it or not, some people are simply afraid to dream again because they tried it and it didn't work the last time. They are scared from past failures and don't want to go through any more disappointments. These people are stuck in Settleville.

You must dream if you are ever going to reach your Next. It's time to take the dream off the shelf and dust it off. You must get back in the game and start believing in yourself enough to dream like you used to. Start dreaming without any limits and get ready for great things to happen for you.

Dreaming without limits means that you are aware of the challenges and difficulties that lie ahead but you also believe in the possibility of reaching your dreams in spite of the opposition that you may face. The key word here is *possibility*. Don't let your circumstances discourage you from dreaming. I'm a dreamer; I love to dream and imagine myself living out the big picture I see in my mind. I am also a realist, meaning I don't get so intoxicated by the dream that I can't see the difficulties it would take to make it happen. With every dream, I make a tough decision to press through every foreseen difficulty and to not give up. It's easier said than done, but it's still very possible to be determined regardless of how things may look.

Dream Like a Kid

One day I was in the playroom with my son and captured a picture of him lifting fake weights above his head. He was wearing a Superman T-shirt, and he had a look on his face as if he were lifting a thousand pounds. That made me think of my childhood years.

As children we were great about dreaming. We thought there was nothing that we couldn't do. We were superheroes with superpowers, a cape (a towel tied around our neck), and a super imagination that caused us to perform extraordinary acts of strength and courage, like leaping from the sofa to the love seat in the living room.

In all actuality, it wasn't the towel wrapped around your neck that empowered you; it was your belief that all things were possible that fueled your imagination. But somewhere along the way we were taught to put our fantasies and make-believe worlds aside and grow up. Unfortunately, life circumstances took a toll and reduced our imagination of superpowers and belief in ourselves to a mediocre mind-set that says, "There's no way I can do that." Failures, setbacks, and misfortunes have caused us to lose—or at least cover up—the childlike faith we once had. We've convinced ourselves that certain dreams we had are just not humanly possible. But that couldn't be further from the truth.

If that's your mind-set, then you need to change it immediately if you are planning on reaching your Next. Start believing again. Start reaching again. Start acting like a superhero once again. It's time to bring back some of that childlike optimism!

Let me encourage the "grown-up you" to have a talk with the "child you" about your dreams, goals, and desires. I bet the kid inside would say, "It's time to put on your cape and up, up, and away!"

Next Your Way to Success

Once you make a decision to get unstuck and figure out where you really are in your stage of life, opportunities will open up for you to dream again. It will be time to start nexting your way into your future. That's right, I said *nexting*; it creates a momentum and energy in you that will sustain you in the now, while you take the steps to reach the next big thing in your life.

> **Nexting:** the act of dreaming, visualizing,
> equipping, educating, and preparing for
> the "next big thing" in your future.

For now, let's focus on dreaming and visualizing in the beginning stage of reaching your future. Visualize yourself taking the necessary next steps to get you from where you are to where you desire to be.

Vision Is Everything

Years ago when my siblings and I were children, our family went on many fishing trips to Bay City, Texas. On one particular trip, my dad caught a tiny little fish and gave it to my older sister in a small can so she could hold it. That became her little pet fish for the day.

As the day went on, she spilled some water out of the can and decided to walk down to the edge of the bank and get some more water for her fish. She didn't realize that the banks were slippery and after just a few steps, she slipped right in and under the water. No one could see her and panic ensued. It was like trying to find a needle in a haystack. Everyone ran to the water's edge and looked for her with no clear direction of where she was. We saw her fall in, but she was completely submerged and the water was dark.

Then all of sudden we saw a hand with a can in it come up out of the water. That's right, the same can that my dad had given her for her small fish. That small, simple tin can brought vision to my dad. It gave him a sense of possibility. He was able to focus on it and was determined to reach it. That can brought the energy and stamina he needed to fight through the current and save his baby girl from drowning that day.

If you can't see it, you will never be it.

That's exactly what a dream and vision can do for you. It will empower you during difficult times in your life when things get a little challenging. Make no mistake about it: there will be times when you will feel like giving up in the midst of it. All hell will break loose and come against you. Whatever happens, don't stop dreaming. Your dream is the fuel that propels you further in the midst of trying times. Vision can empower you when you feel like you can't go on.

Having a Hill of a Time

One day I went for my usual jog in the neighborhood, but this time, I had the kids with me in the double stroller. I was jogging while pushing around about eighty extra pounds that day.

There's a huge hill toward the end of my jogging route that always brings about a more-than-challenging moment. I think about that terrible hill during the entire jog. I dread it because it drains almost every ounce of energy that I have left.

This particular day when I was making the corner to approach the hill, I decided to focus my mind on a dream of mine instead of on the negative thoughts I usually have while approaching the hill. I began to focus on the next thing for my life. Instead of focusing on how I was going to make it up the hill, I envisioned myself accomplishing my goal of being healthy and in shape.

- I began to envision myself at my ideal weight.
- I saw myself fitting into those new jeans hanging in my closet with the price tag still attached because they were too tight.
- I saw myself having enough energy to play with my children and not get tired.
- I saw myself feeling better and looking better.

Before I knew it, I was at the top of the hill with more than enough energy to cruise on to the end of my jogging route!

Your hill today may be a job that you feel stuck in or a stage of life in which you feel like the hamster on a wheel going nowhere. Maybe you feel like your Next sits on top of a mile-high hillside and it will take every ounce of energy to arrive there.

The truth is you're probably right. It will take every ounce of energy to get there, but your dream and vision will be like rocket fuel to a jet engine and will push you beyond your limitations.

Start Dreaming Again

Once you're ready to start dreaming again, you'll need to set the stage for your success both physically and emotionally.

Physical Place

Find a place that brings out your creativity and imagination, a place that allows you to clear your mind for a period of time and create a blank canvas. This should be a place that removes you from your everyday routine and surroundings.

Some of my favorite places to dream are hillsides, elaborate hotel lobbies, and golf courses with beautiful scenery. Yours may be local parks, museums, or coffee shops.

START DREAMING AGAIN · 89

Emotional Place

Along with a physical place, you'll also need to create some brain space devoted specifically to your dream. So turn off the cell phone and TV, step away from social media, and get away by yourself for a few minutes to a few hours. Find a nice, calm, happy place where you can think uninterrupted.

For me this happens at night when we put the kids down for bed. I'll take a few minutes to sit in a dark, quiet room in the house and just meditate. It also happens when I go for a run. Running clears my mind, and I spend lots of focused energy just thinking about my next steps in pursuing my dreams.

Find the locations or activities that inspire you and bring a sense of calm. Then make the most of it!

Chapter 11

DITCHING THE ROUTINE

Before I dive headfirst into this chapter, I want to start by saying that there are some routines that are good and beneficial for you. For instance, I have an exercise routine I implement four to five times per week. I've been doing this for years and don't plan on changing it significantly unless I no longer see results. This is a well-established routine that gives me a visible return on my investment.

Some people have work routines that enable them to be productive throughout their workweek. They attribute their success to the daily routines in the workplace. Once again, that type of routine gives them a visible return on their investment.

The routines I want to address are those that are getting you nowhere or no longer working for your current life. If what you are currently doing hasn't gotten you any closer to your dream, or if your routine has caused stagnation, then it may be time for a change or new plan of action. That's right, you have to start trying something new in order to get from where you are to where you want to be in life.

Look at it this way: it wouldn't make any sense for a football team to run the same play over and over for an entire game. The opposing team would catch on soon to their routine and stop the progress of the team for the rest of the game. The reason they have many plays in the playbook is because they know that they have to call different plays in order to advance the ball down the field. They have to switch up the routine in order to win.

Let's face it, if what you've done in the past hasn't worked, then it might be time to take a different approach. Don't be afraid to try something new in your life. A new plan will work if you work it!

Creating a New Romance Routine

When my wife Heather and I first met, we discovered that we both had pretty bad track records when it came to past dating relationships. Both of us had our fair share of failed relationships. We had established patterns over the course of our relationships that always ended the same way—we failed. Other people were hurt. Emotions were a mess.

This time around, we knew we needed to take a different approach to dating because we did not want to encounter another relationship going bad. In short, even though we were both in our midthirties, we created a new game plan and approached our dating differently than the way we had done it in the past; that included switching up our former dating routines.

We were pretty much set in our ways, but we knew that our mind-sets would have to change if we wanted to adopt some new dating ideas that we believed would lead to better results. Then we took the next step and set boundaries for our relationship. We had a curfew—yes, a curfew!—and rules in place that would keep us from overnight sleepovers and sex before marriage, since that was important to both of us this time around. We also had accountability partners to provide advice and check to see if we were staying true to our commitments.

This new plan and dating mind-set worked well, and we have

been happily married for years now and have two beautiful children. We also wrote a book about our dating experience called *Dating in Black & White*. But what I want you to understand most from our example is that if you want a different result, you will need a different plan of action.

> Insanity is doing the same thing over and over again and expecting different results. —Albert Einstein

Breaking the Cycle of Boredom

Routines can become boring over time. There is nothing worse than living a boring life day in and day out, doing the same old thing over and over. Boredom has a tendency to lead to worse things like depression, especially if you feel like you are stuck in a rut and you don't see any light at the end of the tunnel.

Some people don't even realize that they are creatures of habit unless someone else points it out. They go to the same restaurants and order the same thing over and over, even though there are many other items on the menu that they would probably enjoy if they just ventured out and tried something new. Their typical excuse is often: "I know what I like, so why would I try something else that I might not like as much?" But that's a pessimistic way of looking at it. What if they try something else and find they like it even more than what they have been ordering? You don't leave room for new positive experiences when you stick to your old tried-and-true preferences.

Doing something new is totally in your control, and it can be fun! You can start today by deciding to do some new things in your life.

- Go to a new restaurant and order something you've never had before.

- Take a different route to work and enjoy the new scenery.

- Reach out and start a new friendship with someone. New connections always have a way of introducing you to new things. This is a must-do!

- Join a club or small group that puts you around a new set of people.

- Challenge yourself to get out of your comfort zone on a daily basis.

- Put a new activity on your calendar at least once a week and follow through in doing it.

Do whatever you need to do in order to break the cycle of routine in your life. Every day you wake up is a brand-new day just waiting for you to experience its newness!

Reinventing Your Routines

Take a moment to identify the routines in your life. Some are still producing great results, and some have become stale and undesired patterns that are draining your physical and emotional energy. Remember, don't try to change everything about your life all at once. When you've created your list of routines that need to be changed, create an action step for each item that will force you to break out of the norm in that particular area of your life. The key to your success in this will be whether or not you actually follow through with what you said you were going to do.

Chapter 12

NARROWING
THE FOCUS

Once you have figured out what it is that you want to do, you'll need to focus your time, energy, and willpower around that one specific thing. Some people busy themselves with running after every idea that pops into their minds, and that is nothing but a distracting road. If you try to do everything at once, you will never get anything done at all. Other people will spend their energy on trying to be something that they are not, or worse, trying to be someone that they are not. We discussed these dream distractions earlier in the book. They will keep you from reaching your dream and exhaust your energy levels.

The person who chases two rabbits catches neither.
—Confucius

First things first—you need to figure out what you want your Next to be. Or at least figure out what you are feeling a pull toward doing. The very thing that you gravitate toward could be a part of your Next. So be aware of your interests, desires, and passions.

You don't have to have every detail worked out and be able to explain every step-by-step action you will take to get there. Details can come later, but you at least need to be headed in the right direction.

The task of figuring out what you want to do with your life is different for everyone. I'll use my personal journey of discovery as an example.

Feeling the Pull, Finding the Focus

Working in ministry for many years, my responsibilities have varied and I have worn many hats. I've done everything from cleaning church toilets to delivering the Sunday morning message. But it wasn't until a few years ago that I really began to focus on my next steps.

As is typical for me, I began feeling a sense of discontentment and knew there was something more. I was happily married with two kids. I was successful in my role as an associate pastor in a wonderful church. But I started feeling that same old pull or yearning that usually indicated a shift or change in my life. When I began to focus on it, I realized that over a period of time, my personal mission of encouraging and inspiring people to reach their dreams had turned into me overseeing programs and the daily administration of certain ministry areas of the church. Now, this was not a bad thing. In fact, this is what fosters health in any organization. My problem was that it had consumed all my time and emotional energy to where I didn't have anything left to give in the form of inspiring others.

I started paying attention to all the things I did that brought me joy, fulfillment, and a sense of purpose. I also started pinpointing all the things I was doing that were starting to suck the very life right out of me. Now here is where the focus part really matters. In order for you to gain a sense of the right direction to move toward, it's important for you to have an awareness of your passions, strengths, and weaknesses.

I knew my passion was to inspire, encourage, and motivate people. I live for that! One of the main reasons I know that is my passion is because I never get tired of doing it. I love helping people discover their purpose; I love being a motivator in their lives. One of the ways I am passionate about inspiring others is through speaking. I'm fortunate that the stage has been my platform for many years and it has always been a joy and delight to share a message of hope, inspiration, and encouragement with an audience.

Another way I enjoy being a source of inspiration is through my writing. I began to focus more on my writing, but my passion alone wasn't an indicator that I was focused on the right thing or headed in the right direction. I needed evidence that my writing mattered, and people are a great source of unsolicited feedback. I began to compile all the emails, social media posts, and text messages I received from people who either heard me speak or read one of my blog posts, and I began to look for commonality in their messages and feedback. To my surprise, the majority of them were people thanking me for encouraging and inspiring them to go after their dreams. I even went back and listened to several of my older messages and identified a key statement that I made in many of them. That key statement always came in the form of a question I would ask the audience, usually at the beginning of the message. The question was, "How many of you are ready to go from where you are to where you want to be?" That was my big aha moment. It suddenly all made sense. I knew I was on the right track.

Laser-like focus helps me keep the main thing the main thing. It also prevents me from trying to do everything. I'm sure you've heard the old label, "Jack of all trades and master of none." That is usually what happens when you lack focus. You end up trying to do way too much, and unfortunately it reduces your efforts and effectiveness to a minimum. Focus enables you to stay in your lane like a runner and not be distracted by other things that you could be doing.

It's time for you to figure out those areas and endeavors that you need to focus on. Your ability to focus is the very thing that will empower you to keep moving in the direction of your dreams. It will empower you to cut through the adversity and ups and downs that you will no doubt encounter on your journey.

Focus Creates Energy

My wife and I take TaeBo classes, and it's a very exhausting yet fulfilling workout. One of the things the instructors taught us when we first started taking the classes is that you have to keep your mind focused even when your body starts getting tired. They told us that if our mind wandered, then our bodies would follow, and the temptation to quit would bombard us. They were absolutely right, and that's exactly what happened to me the first few times I was in the class. The moment I got tired, my mind wandered and started thinking about quitting and walking out.

One of the things the instructors did to help us stay focused was to put padded, red mitts on their hands and stand in front of us during punching and kicking routines. The mitt was called a "focus mitt," and it certainly did what it was supposed to do. Every time they came around and stood in front of me, a burst of energy would come from deep within me as I focused on executing the techniques and connecting my punches and kicks with the focus mitt. That focus mitt reminded me of why I was there in the first place, and that was to reach my goal of being healthy and physically fit. It was very effective and served as a great teaching lesson for me as well.

Let your dream and passion serve as your focus mitt. Let it remind you of why you are on the journey to your Next. Let it keep your mind focused during those times you want to quit. Keep your focus strong, and get ready for those bursts of energy that will keep you moving forward in pursuit of your Next.

Next Steps to Narrowing Your Focus

Think of two to three things you need to focus on in the days ahead that will cause you to make progress toward your goal. Please do not focus on more than one goal at a time. If you try to focus on ten goals or dreams all at once, you will never get anything done.

Once you've identified one goal and a few areas of focus, make sure to write them down and put them in an area where you will see them every day. For example:

- Put them on a dry erase board in your office.
- Put them on your bathroom mirror.
- Make them the home screen on your computer or mobile phone and review them a few times each day.

Chapter 13

PREVAILING OVER PROCRASTINATION

Procrastination is an invisible force that has the power to keep you from ever advancing toward your Next. It can stop you in your tracks, all the while giving you the illusion that you are making progress because you are still thinking about doing it *some day*. You spend hours imagining yourself living your dream, but for some reason you are not doing anything to get there. You keep putting off doing those daily, weekly, and monthly action steps that are designed to get you closer to your destination. Before you know it, your dream has drifted farther and farther away and you are exhausted just thinking about all the things you have to do to get there.

Don't get in the habit of saying, "I'll get to that tomorrow." Sooner or later you will realize that when tomorrow shows up, you'll feel overwhelmed with a growing to-do list and not enough time. And what will that make you want to do? Put it off until tomorrow!

Lessons in Laundry

My wife and I experienced this with one of our weekly house chores. When it came time to do laundry, we had a tendency to wash a load of clothes but would never fold them on the same day that we washed them. We would just place them in a basket and say, "I'll get to that tomorrow." Several days would pass, and we would have baskets of clothes stacked in our room, which became a big eyesore and constant reminder of our procrastination. When we got sick and tired of walking by the baskets of clothes, we would move them into our closet just to get them out of sight. Ridiculous, I know, but that's what we did. Needless to say, that process didn't work. The nagging feeling just wouldn't let us rest. Finally, after pushing through and folding several baskets of laundry in one day, we came to an agreement and found a solution that would keep us from procrastinating in this area. We simply made it a rule that whenever someone does a load of laundry, they must fold it on the same day. This kept us from procrastinating and eliminated a buildup of laundry baskets in our room.

You may think that's a silly story, but a lot of people spend their lives exactly like this. They are excited about the idea of reaching their dreams, but for some reason they put off doing those things they need to be doing in order to get there. They convince themselves that they will start tomorrow. They imagine themselves doing it, but in reality they never get to it because they are always coming up with excuses of why today is not the right day to start. If that sounds like you, then make a decision to stop procrastinating right now. There is no one keeping you from starting the task or project but you.

Just Do It!

A while back I had an idea to start doing some video blogs, otherwise known as *vlogging*. I wanted to make some motivating and inspiring videos, especially since encouraging others is a huge passion of mine. I had always liked making videos and thought this was a great idea. I also had the experience to execute this idea:

- I was already accustomed to making videos and being on camera.
- I had the necessary equipment to get started.
- It was a project that didn't require a lot of my time.

But for some reason I just kept putting it off. I kept saying to myself that one day I was going to start recording the videos, but that day never came. It wasn't until I realized that *I* was the only thing between me and achieving my goal. No one was stopping me or in my way but *me*.

Procrastination was certainly getting the best of me and stopping my progress. So I decided to prevail over procrastination by simply starting to do what I had been thinking about doing all along. *It was that simple.* I set up the camera and pushed record. I forced myself to get in front of the camera and start talking. I quit looking for the perfect time and decided that *this was* the perfect time. I did it and enjoyed it! I just couldn't believe it took me that long to actually do it.

Imagine all the ideas you've had that you never took action on because you kept putting it off. Those ideas could have been the very thing to get you closer to your dream, but you never found the time to start. Or maybe you were just looking for the *perfect time* to start. Some people can't see it's the perfect time now because they're too busy looking for it in the future.

Start today and make it the perfect time to do those things you have been thinking about doing. Start putting some action to those ideas and win over procrastination. Right now is the perfect time.

Kick Procrastination to the Curb

Stop right now and take inventory of your to-do list. Start identifying the items on your list that you know you *should be doing* but for some reason you haven't started doing them. Once you've identified those items, then it's time to take the first step and actually start doing them. Start right now with what you have. Do whatever you have to do in order to get yourself moving in the right direction. If you're not motivated, then get motivated! Think of all the ways your life will improve when you finally do that one thing. And when you've finished it, move to the next item on the list.

A lack of motivation can be caused by either emotional or physical circumstances. When I hit a wall and start feeling a little less motivated, I always take a quick look at my life patterns from the last few weeks. Maybe I've been burning the midnight oil on a couple of projects that I'm working on. The problem with that is the default of eating unhealthy fast food because it's easy, staying up too late, and not getting enough rest. This results in my body being tired and sluggish and my mind not functioning at its peak due to sleep deprivation. Once I make some simple adjustments—eating healthy food and going to sleep at a reasonable hour—then I am back up and running with fresh energy and more motivation to continue on.

Always be aware of what demotivates you. That will empower you to quickly make necessary adjustments to get back to a life full of energy.

A great source of motivation and inspiration for me when it comes to prevailing over procrastination is to visualize several baskets of unfolded laundry piling up in my bedroom. Just the mere thought of that sucks the life right out of me now! By applying that simple thought to other areas of my life, it actually motivates me to be more action oriented versus always putting things off.

Remember, the longer you put things off, the more things pile up on your to-do list. Pretty soon, your list will be so long that it seems impossible to accomplish.

You can't afford to let procrastination prevail over you any longer. Pick an item on your list and just do it!

PART III

FACING FEAR HEAD-ON

"The only thing we have to fear is fear itself."
—Franklin D. Roosevelt

Just because fear is present doesn't mean that confidence is not. Fear will always be the enemy between you and your dream of accomplishing something great. It will haunt you and taunt you every chance it gets. But you can always be victorious.

Most people, if they are honest, will admit that they fear at least one thing in their lives. Even successful people have fears, but the difference with them is that they never let their fears stop them from reaching their dreams. They simply act anyway. And once they take steps toward their dream, the fear subsides.

If you are going to get to your Next, then you too will have to learn to look your fears in the eye and decide to keep moving forward, no matter how scared you might be.

Chapter 14

CONQUERING REJECTION

E ven the most confident people in the world have struggled at one time or another with overcoming rejection. The fear of rejection often keeps people from taking any step at all in the direction of their Next. They don't want to be hurt, let down, or disappointed, so they stay in the so-called safe zone of Settleville, that boring place we talked about earlier.

Love on the Links

When I first met my wife, I was absolutely terrified to let her know I liked her. I acted like I had all the confidence in the world, so it seemed like it should have been easy to approach her and ask her out, but I was afraid of being rejected. I went so far as to create one of those so-called safe zones that would eliminate the risk of rejection.

When I found out she liked to play golf, I started a golf life group at my church. I approached her nonchalantly and said, "Hey Heather, I heard you liked to play golf, and I wanted to let you know that I have a golf life group here at church. Now if you just give me your number and email, I can let you know when the group is going to play." Clever, right? That was a safe way for me to get her contact information without letting on that I was interested in her.

It did get me out on the course with her and other golfers, but I still hadn't told her I was interested. I finally realized that I was going to have to get over my fear of rejection if I was ever going to get anywhere with her. Guess what? When I finally told her I was interested, I was thrilled to find out that she was too.

Rejection Resistance

You will never move forward if you are afraid of rejection by others. Some people never go for more because they fear they will be told they don't qualify or have the credentials. But don't accept no as the final answer.

I have a friend who worked at a mall kiosk to help pay his way through school. He was one of the workers in the mall that you shamelessly try to avoid while walking past them, desperately trying to avoid any type of eye contact or body language that would possibly suggest that you are interested in what they are offering. You walk by them hoping that they don't ask you if you have a second or if you would like to try their product.

I remember asking him one day how he dealt with many people turning him down when he tried to extend an invitation to demonstrate or showcase the product. He laughed and said, "At first it was hard and intimidating, but then I learned a few tips to conquering the fear of rejection that helped me along the way." I was intrigued!

Here are the tips my friend taught me that day.

1. Rejection is not the end-all.

Rejection is bound to happen to all of us at one time or another. It's a part of life. But just because you've been turned down doesn't mean it's the end for you. Never let one rejection discourage you from one more try. My friend learned that if he was ever going to be successful, he would have to be resilient and couldn't take rejection personally.

2. Never expect rejection, and always expect the best.

After so many rejections in the beginning, my friend quickly came to expect it. What he didn't realize was that expecting rejection was affecting his sales pitch. He lost confidence in his delivery because he feared one more person avoiding him. Once he realized what was happening, he changed his mind-set. Instead of expecting the worst, he began to expect the best every time he stopped a potential customer in the mall. By expecting the best, it caused him to perform at his best, and in the end, it resulted in sales and great interaction with customers.

3. There is always tomorrow.

Sometimes believing this was easier said than done, but it kept him going. No matter if things didn't go the way he thought they would, at the end of his workday, he would drive home thinking about how tomorrow was going to be a better day.

These tips worked for my friend during that season of his life, and eventually he went on to do bigger things. But he will always have that great experience of learning how to overcome rejection, and it will serve him well the rest of his life, no matter the situation.

Fear of rejection is like anything else: the only way to conquer it is to face it and experience it head-on.

Rejecting Rejection

Rejection will happen. The way you respond to it will either set you up for failure or set you up for success. You can walk away feeling hopeless, or you can walk away with hope for tomorrow by repeating simple words of encouragement to yourself at the very moment you feel rejected.

Come up with about three life-giving, encouraging statements to ward off any feelings of rejection you encounter while on the way to your Next. Make sure you memorize those statements or put them in a place where they are easily accessible, like your smartphone, so that you will be ready to encourage yourself whenever needed. Be proactive so when that time comes for you, you will be prepared to overcome it and you won't be fumbling for a reaction. You got this!

Chapter 15

NO RISK, NO REWARD

A friend of mine was driving around with his father-in-law one day, and they passed a neighborhood that was filled with expensive homes. My friend said out loud, "Wow, I wonder what kind of careers the people who live in these homes have." His father-in-law had a different perspective and said, "I wonder what kind of huge risks those people took to get where they are now." People who succeed are not always rich or lucky; they are risk takers. Risk must be embraced if anyone is going to take a step of faith toward his or her dreams. If you're not naturally a risk taker, then it's time to push yourself to the edge and jump.

The greater the risk, the greater the reward.

If you could see the end result beforehand, then it wouldn't be a risk at all, and it wouldn't take much to get there. Just because you can't see your future doesn't mean you don't have one. Like I mentioned earlier, you don't have to have it all figured out. Sometimes all you really need is clarity for the next step that you are supposed to take. So do yourself a favor and stop trying to figure it all out. The truth is, you will never have it *all* figured out.

How many times have you felt like you should be doing something that you're not currently doing, but you talked yourself out of it? It happens more often than not. It's no fun living your life with thoughts of "I shoulda, coulda, woulda" constantly haunting your mind. Here are a few reasons why some people fail to take the leap of faith:

1. They think about it too long.

Thinking about doing something is different than actually doing it. Don't get stuck in a thought process of trying to figure everything out. As my grandma used to say, "If you think long, you think wrong." Usually when you think about something too long, you will have a tendency to talk yourself out of doing it before you even get started. Or you spend all your time fantasizing about living your dream instead of actually doing what needs to be done in order to start living it in reality.

As a great example of this, there's a very intense scene in the movie *Collateral* starring Tom Cruise and Jamie Foxx. Tom plays Vincent, a cool, calm assassin, and Jamie plays Max, the cab driver, whom Vincent forces to drive him around the city to the destination of each of his targets.

Throughout the movie, Vincent and Max have multiple conversations. One of the conversations includes a dream that Max has of owning his own limousine company. Max has a picture of the limousine in his cab and says that driving the cab is just a temporary thing until he reaches his dream. Max admits he even went so far as to convince his mom that he was actually living his dream when in reality, he is far from it.

In one scene, Max confronts Vincent and questions his morality because of what he does for a living. Vincent then turns on

Max and begins to confront him for never having the guts to go after his dream of owning his own limousine company. The look on Max's face is an expression of utter realization that Vincent is right—he isn't doing anything to get himself closer to making his life's dream his reality. It's a look produced by honest dialogue with himself as he listens to Vincent's words.

Here are the actual lines from Vincent to Max in the movie—with a little editing, due to the language:

> Someday? Someday my dream will come? One night you will wake up and discover it never happened. It's all turned around on you. It never will. Suddenly you are old. Didn't happen, and it never will, because you were never going to do it anyway. You'll push it into memory and then zone out in your barco lounger, being hypnotized by daytime TV for the rest of your life … What the [heck] are you still doing driving a cab?

Vincent is trying to get Max to see that he needs to put action to his dream and make it happen because it isn't going to happen all by itself.

Maybe you've found yourself stuck in the same situation for years, only dreaming about a brighter tomorrow. If so, take a moment right now and ask yourself this one question—and then answer it truthfully. *What the heck am I still doing driving a cab?*

Sometimes we need a reality check to slap us
in the face and wake us up from dreaming
so we can actually start doing.

---

2. They can't see what's ahead.

If you're not a fortune-teller, that's perfectly okay. Just because you can't see the future doesn't mean you don't have one. Taking a leap of faith doesn't mean you see the big picture in advance. Sometimes all you can see is a small glimpse. Personally, I'd rather see a small glimpse than no glimpse at all.

Reaching your Next will sometimes require you to step outside of your comfort zone. It will require you to keep moving forward even when you can't see your future.

> Faith is taking the first step even when you
> can't see the whole staircase. —Martin Luther King Jr.

One day I was driving to my TaeBo class early in the morning and was met with an unexpected dense fog that immediately slowed my progress. The fog was so thick that you could cut it with a knife. I was familiar with the road since I drive it at least three to four times a week, but with the heavy fog it felt as if I was driving in uncharted territory. Not seeing ahead made me a little nervous. In all reality the road was still there, but there's something about not seeing where you're going that causes just enough doubt to make you second-guess your situation.

So I slowed down but continued moving forward to my destination. And a few minutes later, I exited the fog.

On your journey to your destiny, dream, or goal, sometimes the road gets a little foggy ahead. That's not the time to stop but to keep moving forward. It's okay if you slow down just a little while you build your confidence and maintain your belief, but by all means, don't ever stop moving.

3. They allow fear to stop them in their tracks.

No one ever said that taking a leap of faith isn't scary at times. In fact, having a little fear is a great indicator that you are about to do something that is much bigger than you. Don't be afraid of the unknown; it just might surprise you yet. Go ahead and take the leap and enjoy the journey.

My friend Steve told me his story one day. He is a successful businessman who took a huge risk to get where he is today. He had been working for a company for several years when he started feeling that it was time for him to take a next step and start his own business. This was a huge risk for him. He was married with children, and this next step would be a risk for all of them. There would be no guarantee of a regular paycheck. He would risk being without the amenities that he and his family had grown accustomed to, like food, clothing, health insurance, and a roof over your head. But his feeling didn't go away. Instead, it grew stronger.

When he finally took the risk and made the step toward his Next, he and his family were hit with some trying times. He had his business in his home and worked hard every day making cold calls, marketing, and advertising his services. There were even times when he would sit and stare at the phone and fax machine, hoping for a future client to reach out to him. In the end, the phone rang, the fax machine fired up, and his business began to take off. In fact, Steve told me his story from his high-rise office with a huge window overlooking the city. Once again, his story is proof that the bigger the risk, the bigger the reward.

> The most difficult thing is the decision to act;
> the rest is merely tenacity. —Amelia Earhart

Make the Move

Moving from Texas to Nashville nearly ten years ago was one of the toughest decisions of my life. Leaving family and friends and moving out to a different state was beyond scary. I packed up everything I owned in my SUV and hit the road. It was the best of times and it was the worst of times. I had no job, nor the promise of one. All I had was that gut feeling that there was something much more for my life than what I was currently experiencing. I knew that moving to Nashville was the next step for me, but that's all I knew. It was truly a step of faith and with huge risks:

- A risk of not finding a job.
- A risk of being stuck again.
- A risk of being alone in a new place.

I ended up living with a roommate from the new church I attended. I stayed in his extra bedroom and had no furniture of my own; I slept on an air mattress for months. I started working for a carpet cleaning company as a way to bring in some income since I was beginning to drain my savings account. Still, I never lost faith or the vision for more for my life. I refused to stay stuck and kept moving forward to the next thing.

Now years later I have a beautiful wife, two amazing kids, and a life that brings such fulfillment. I'm so glad I took the risk, and you will be glad about the risks that you take as well. Get ready for great things to happen for you. All you need to do is step out in order to find out.

Risk for Your Reward

Risk is like working out your muscles. When you first begin taking risks, it can be a little painful, but the more you do it, the easier it becomes.

Think about some of your next steps that are huge risks. It's important that you don't just jump off the cliff headfirst without counting the cost. Take some time to think about all the other people and areas of your life that this next decision will impact in one way or another. This will allow you to gain a much larger perspective and empower you to methodically think through everything in advance.

Chapter 16

IT'S SCARY OUT THERE!

here is always a little fear when stepping out into the unknown. You may face fear of failure because you just aren't sure what's out there—but this is a good place to be. It will stretch you, and without a doubt challenge you, and will ultimately make you better.

If you are serious about getting to the next thing for your life, you will have to learn to beat any fears that have the potential to stop you in your tracks. Your Next will not be handed to you on a silver platter, nor will it just magically happen without being challenged by the forces of fear. You have to stare fear in the face and not back down.

> Courage is being scared to death but saddling up anyway.
> —John Wayne

The Academy Award–winning movie *The Shawshank Redemption* gives a clear picture of what fear can do to a person. The main character, Andy, played by Tim Robbins, is an innocent man who ends up in prison. He is there for many years, and during that time he makes a small group of friends.

Andy is determined that prison is not his final resting place and that there is more for him. He devises a well-thought-out plan of escape and carries out the steps of breaking free over the course of several years. While his eyes are set on freedom, there are others in his small group of friends who have been incarcerated for so long that they can't imagine an outside world, nor the thought of living in it, for fear that they wouldn't know how to survive on the outside. The very thought of Andy wanting to be free and live outside of the prison is foreign to them. They have become institutionalized.

Although Andy finally escapes, his friends are stuck in a fear-driven mind-set. There's a heartbreaking scene in which an old prisoner is up for parole but the fear of the outside drives him to break out in a behavior that causes the prison board to revoke his parole. He was literally moments away from freedom but was afraid because he didn't know what was waiting for him beyond the prison doors.

The Other Side of Fear

As I think about that movie, it reminds me of my Uncle Samuel. Samuel grew up in a small town right outside of Houston, Texas. He was the biggest, baddest, loudest man in town, and he went by the nickname "Little Sam." He was tough as nails and wasn't afraid of anybody. Everybody in town knew not to mess with him. As a little kid it made me feel pretty big when I would go visit him and other extended family during the summer. I would see people point at me and hear them whisper, "That's Little Sam's nephew."

Sam was also an expert when it came to shooting a rifle. He could shoot a rat running through a field with a BB gun. He also had a drinking problem. He couldn't hold down a full-time job and was never able to sustain a successful relationship. He was nice to his relatives and would give you the shirt off his back, but for some reason he never could get his life together.

When he passed away several years ago after having a massive heart attack and organ failure as a result of constant drinking and drugs, I went to be with the family for the funeral. As the family sat around telling stories about Little Sam, I asked my mother, "Why in the world did he never change to better his life?" Her answer changed my whole perspective.

Uncle Samuel wasn't always like that. Early in his life, he was in the military. He excelled during his training and was considered an expert marksman when it came to weapons and artillery. This was during the time of the Vietnam War, and many soldiers were about to get their next assignment. My uncle Samuel was afraid that his next orders were going to send him to Vietnam. He was so overcome with fear that he went AWOL before he even received his orders. When the military finally caught up with him, right before he was dishonorably discharged, they told him what his next assignment would have been. Fear of the unknown had totally convinced him that he was headed to Vietnam, but the army actually had plans to send him to Washington to help train other soldiers in marksmanship.

The news crushed his spirit, and he never recovered from the thought of what he could have been. That one moment changed his life forever. I truly believe his life would have turned out differently if he would have looked fear in the face and stood his ground. He could still be alive today, living a productive life of purpose and fulfillment.

Everything you've ever wanted is on the other side of fear.

—George Addair

I use that story to point out the fact that you won't know everything that is waiting for you, but that's not a good reason to not go after your dream, nor is it a good reason to run from any fears you have.

Maybe you feel as if you let a major opportunity pass you by because you were too afraid. Maybe you've found yourself slowly slipping into a life of regret. If that's you, then stop right now. There's *always* a second chance. Just because you miss one opportunity doesn't mean that another one won't come around.

I wish my uncle Samuel would have been able to bounce back and keep his head up after that disappointing news. I wish he wouldn't have gone AWOL in the first place. But after being discharged, he was so busy looking at the missed opportunity that it distracted him from seeing any new ones that surely would have come his way.

> It's never too late to be what you might have been.
> —George Eliot

Missed Opportunities

Some people believe that missed opportunities never come back around. That couldn't be any further from the truth. If you feel as if you've missed an opportunity somewhere in your past that will never come back to you, then it's time to change that belief.

Make a list of the missed opportunities that still weigh heavy on your mind. Now write out a plan of action for each one that will get you on the path of making it a reality. If you can successfully write out a step-by-step plan of action, the opportunity is likely still available for you, even if it looks a little different now. Allow yourself to get excited about these opportunities all over again!

Chapter 17

EXPOSING EXCUSES

T he most destructive force against your dream is your excuses. Don't let your excuses sabotage your future. Excuses are dream killers and progress stoppers. Some people even use them as a safeguard so they won't have to take a step of faith and try something new. The only thing that lies between them and their destiny is the barricade of excuses that they have placed on the road themselves.

> You can make excuses, or you can make progress, but you can't make both.

Have you ever had a dream that never got off the ground because you gave yourself one excuse after another as to why you couldn't or shouldn't? If that's you, then it's time to drop the excuses that are killing your dream and get after it.

Here are eight excuses that could be killing your dream:

1. I don't have the time.

We are given twenty-four hours every day. The truth is you don't have a time-deficiency problem; you have a time-management problem. You will need to prioritize your daily activities and strategically allow a certain amount of time to work toward your goals on a consistent basis. If you have time for television and social media, then you have time to work on your dream.

> People who are living their dreams are
> the people who made time for their dreams.

Let's face it, when there is something that we really want, we will do whatever we have to do in order to make time for it. If you are really ready for your Next, then you must get rid of this excuse once and for all.

When my wife and I wrote our first book together, we both had our own careers and were also parents to a three-year-old and a one-year-old. Our lives were already busy when we added "writing a book" to our schedules.

In the beginning, we wrote whenever a free moment came up, and those times were few and far between. We had certain deadlines set and were on a schedule with our editor, but as the days went by we found ourselves using the excuse that we just didn't have enough time. We were busy at work and then busy at home with our children, so that was a legitimate excuse, right? Nope, wrong answer. The bottom line is that excuses always stop progress.

We got frustrated with writing and with one another as time went on. Then we made a shift. We realized that we did have enough time; all we needed to do was shift some of our priorities for a period of time. For example, every evening after putting the kids down for bed, we would normally watch one of our favorite TV shows to have some alone time. But we decided that for several weeks we would write during that time instead of watching our favorite shows. We realized the power of replacement. If you are going to add an activity to your already busy schedule, then you must be willing to let it replace an existing activity.

Yes, we valued our alone time together, but we were also focused on the short-term goal of submitting our rough draft to our editor. Even with our busy schedules, this gave us all the time we needed. The power of replacement allowed us to reach our goal, and it wasn't long before we were back to watching our favorite TV shows together.

2. I don't have the ability.

The very fact that you are dreaming about it proves that you are equipped with the raw talent to get you started. You *do have* what it takes. Just get started, and the ability you thought you didn't have will show up along the way. Oftentimes it's the very challenge of reaching your Next that will bring out the ability and courage you thought you never had. There will also be times when a great friend or mentor will be the instrument that helps bring out that super person in you.

Friday is usually my off day, and I spend it with my kids while my wife is at work. Some of our favorite activities are eating at our favorite barbecue restaurant and then going to the park for a few hours. The particular park we go to in our neighborhood has a huge play area. One day, my son, Grayson (who was four years old at the time), attempted to climb the big ladder that led to the tall spiral slide—for the very first time. I stood at the base of the ladder and encouraged him all the way with positive words.

When he reached the top step, he was just one step away from the landing that led to the slide. All of a sudden, fear tried to bombard his mind. He looked down at me and said, "I can't do it, Daddy. I can't do it." I wasn't going to agree with him. Instead I kept on saying, "Yes, you can, son. Yes, you can." Lack of confidence in his own ability caused him to freeze and grip the ladder rail tightly when he was just one step away from success. Because he was just a child, it was up to me to speak to the greatness and the ability that was inside of him the whole time. I explained that he could do it because he was such a big boy and he had already made it up the ladder on his own. Then I said the magic words: "If you do it, we will go and get some ice cream after we leave the park." That did it. The fear went away, and he turned around and made it to the last step that led to success.

This is a great example of why it's so important to hang around positive people. If I had agreed with my son, he never would have moved forward. Instead, he was able to experience a new confidence when he came down the slide.

Most people can overcome their fear; they just don't know it. It's so easy to get stuck in the mind-set of what you can't do, especially when you are faced with obstacles, fears, and limitations. This type of mind-set never allows you to envision yourself actually accomplishing the very thing you desire. When you allow fear to win, it causes you to panic and freak out, and you will talk yourself out of success even when you might be just one step away.

Yes, some of our dreams are so *big* that they frighten us. Some of our goals seem way *beyond* our ability. We all have desires that can appear to be *far* out of our reach. This doesn't mean that you can't; it just means you have to start telling yourself that *you can*.

- If you want more out of life, *you can* have it.

- If you don't like where you are, *you can* change that.

- *You can* punch fear in the face and make your dream a reality.

- *You can* start right now by thinking more positively about your future.

- When things get tough, *you can* still make it.

- When you feel like giving up or quitting, *you can* ignore that feeling and keep moving forward.

- *You can* begin to dream bigger than ever—right now.

Regardless of your current limitation, education, or financial situation, *you can* be successful. This list could go on and on of all the things that *you can do*. If all else fails, you might want to go back and read about the little engine that could: *I think I can. I think I can. I think I can!*

3. I don't have enough education.

Many millionaires and top successful business people never finished high school or even took one semester of college. They didn't allow that to stop them. I'm not insinuating that education is not important, but what I am saying is that the lack of it should not stop you from reaching your dreams. In today's society, social media has made it easy to acquire resources and knowledge from successful people who are already doing what you are dreaming about. Follow them on social media and start learning from them now.

Some of your dreams may require you getting another level of education. But once again, it's up to you to do something about it and quit using your lack of education as an excuse.

4. I might fail.

Success stories are often birthed from a compilation of failures and mistakes. There is life after your mistakes. There is a future beyond your failures. Don't let the fear of failure stop you from accomplishing the dream that's inside you.

> Many of life's failures are people who
> did not realize how close they were to success
> when they gave up. —Thomas Edison

Many times it's not just the fear of failure that stops us, but it is the fear of others seeing our failures that overwhelms us and stops us dead in our tracks. The thought of possible embarrassment can just be too much for us to deal with, and we don't want to take that chance. This is where you need to get over the opinions of other people and start realizing that failures can be great teaching moments for you—and for them—along the journey.

Failure is only negative when you fail to learn from it. Then your chances of a repeated failure are much higher. You must quit looking at failure as if it means the end of your dream. Start approaching your failures as if they are teachers that are educating you. See yourself becoming smarter, wiser, and better equipped because of each failure that you encounter along your journey.

5. I don't have enough money.

In reality, some of our dreams do cost us more than hard work and sweat. Sometimes our dreams cost money. Just because you can't afford it now doesn't mean you can't afford it later. Plan, budget, and prepare. People who are serious about their dreams understand that they might have to make a few financial cutbacks now in order to get to their destination tomorrow. When you plan, budget, and make cutbacks, you are preparing the way for you to reach your Next.

When my wife and I got married, she moved into my little

one-bedroom apartment. It was so small you could take one giant step and go from the kitchen to the bedroom. Oh, and did I mention my wife also came with a large Dalmatian dog? You can just imagine how crowded we were in that apartment. We wasted no time and started dreaming of a bigger place.

We knew we wanted kids in our future, and we were certainly not going to have them in that little one-bedroom apartment. We didn't have enough money at the time to buy a house, but we didn't let that stop us. We made an agreement that we would stay in the apartment for at least one full year and then we would start looking for a house.

In the meantime, we started budgeting, which included cutting out unnecessary expenses and eating at home versus going out to dinner all the time. My wife became a pro at couponing. She continues to save us thousands of dollars per year by the mere action of cutting coupons once a week and planning our meals accordingly. We also paid off all of our debt that year and started saving for all the expenses we would incur as new homebuyers.

This took commitment and dedication on our part. Every time we denied ourselves of temporary satisfaction, we would have to remind ourselves of the bigger reward, which was a much bigger home that we could one day raise a family in.

> You should be so passionate about reaching your Next that the thought of obtaining it totally outweighs the sacrifices it takes to get there.

Well, guess what? When the time came for us to purchase and move into our bigger home, we had all the money we needed and then some. In fact, even before we moved into our home, we had already purchased enough furniture (and paid cash) for every room on the first floor.

So if you think you don't have enough money for your dream, I want to encourage you to think again. Create a budget so you can get an overall look at your current financial situation. I encourage you to check out Dave Ramsey's resources. My wife and I have used his resources, and they have done wonders for us in the area of our finances.

It's also time to get creative in finding ways to acquire the finances you need to produce your dream. Start looking at ways you can bring in extra money to start funding your dream. You might be able to put in some overtime at work or even pick up a second part-time job for a period of time.

> Take a few minutes here to write out a list of ways you could start saving or bringing in extra income to resource your dream.

6. I ain't nobody.

If you think this, then you've already started out with a double negative, and that's not good. Humorous or not, this one is the silent killer. You would never say it out loud, but chances are you have thought this a time or two. You've questioned your own ability. "Who am I to think I can do that? Who am I to think I have what it takes?" Then comes that dreadful answer from your own inner voice: "I ain't nobody."

But here's a news flash—*you are somebody*. You do have what it takes. Perhaps your next step is to simply believe in yourself. You must become your greatest source of encouragement and quit comparing yourself to others. Stop feeling inferior. You are the person with the dream. *You* have the desire for more. You will rise to the occasion and become the person who is living the life that you have imagined.

7. I'm too tired.

You don't have an energy problem; you've got a passion problem. When you are passionate about your dreams, then seeing them become a reality will supercharge you. Passion creates an energy that will sustain you on the journey to your destination; it will wake you up early and get you going.

Or maybe it's not a passion problem but a vision problem. Maybe you've reached a place where you are losing sight of the vision of reaching your Next. Trust me, what you see—your vision—has the ability to reenergize you, even when you feel like you can't go on.

To bring home this point, several motivational speakers have shared the following story. While funny and humorous, it is a scenario we can probably all identify with.

> A woman comes home from work tired and exhausted. She tells her husband that it's been a very long and hard day at work and she is way too tired to prepare the family's evening dinner. Then she lies down on the sofa to rest. A few minutes later, the phone rings, and it's her best friend calling to inform her that the red dress that she has been eyeing for a while is finally on sale for half off at their favorite clothing store. The lady who was once tired and exhausted all of a sudden springs into action. She jumps up from the couch, puts on her shoes, kisses her husband bye, and out the door she goes, headed to purchase that red dress.

Was she lying about being tired and exhausted? Was that just an excuse so she wouldn't have to cook dinner? I don't think so. She probably did have a long, exhausting day and was truly too tired to muster up enough energy to prepare dinner.

What happened then? She was energized by the phone call she received from her best friend telling her about the red dress being half off. The vision of her wearing the coveted dress gave her the shot of adrenaline she needed to get off the couch and get moving in the direction of her dream.

The moral of the story is that if you keep your vision alive, you will stay energized enough to reach whatever it is that you've been dreaming about. You may just need to reevaluate your vision from time to time.

8. It's too late for me.

It's never too late to be what you might have been, to get back in the game and get moving toward your destiny. The longer you hold on to that excuse, the further your dream gets away from you. Don't let life pass you by!

I've met many people who decided later in life to take their dreams off the shelf and start believing in them again. Let's face it, when you truly have a dream inside of you, there is nothing you can do to shake off that feeling. It will keep beating within you and will never let you settle for a life less than what you were intended to have.

Melissa's Story

Here's a great story from a woman named Melissa, who conquered her excuses and is now on the path to accomplishing her dreams.

I had been planning a return to school to pursue my master's degree in education ever since I graduated with my bachelor's in 2006, but it seemed that something always got in the way of me taking that step—there was not enough money, not enough time, family issues, and most importantly, a cloudy view of what my course of study should be. Eventually I felt like I was going nowhere and I started to feel stuck.

When I was given leadership positions at work where I was a teacher in a local middle school, instead of using them as a launch pad to what I knew my future was supposed to hold, I began to settle for those little achievements. I thought, "Well, as long as I keep getting recognized, I guess I don't really need that post-grad degree." I was trying to convince myself that I would be okay if I never reached my goal.

You see, I had inquired about several different programs over the years, but nothing seemed quite right, and I was almost at the point of giving up. Then I

heard about a program that seemed to be just what I was looking for, but it didn't match my career path at that time. So I continued on a path that made me miserable, because it was safe.

When I took an executive-level position at my church, suddenly the course of study I had been interested in made perfect sense—but the same old obstacles started to rear their ugly heads again: finances, time, family issues … everything got in the way and convinced me that there was no way I could get it done. I was discouraged again and had begun to think that I would never earn that degree. I was so unhappy that one of my supervisors commented on my facial expressions at work. I hadn't even realized I was unhappy yet, but I was wearing it all over my face!

Then I heard Adonis's message on getting to the "Next" step in life, and it totally changed my perspective. It was so simple, yet so profound. It gave me the inspiration and motivation I needed to move forward, and I'm so glad I did.

The finances are no longer an issue and the schedule is perfect for a busy working mother. I am pleased to say that I began my pursuit of a master's of science in organizational leadership at Our Lady of the Lake University in Spring of 2015. My Next starts now!

What a great story! I love it when real life collides with real people and produces such inspiring examples. No matter where you are in your stage of life, you must always remember that it is never too late to go after those dreams that you thought were too far out of your reach. Let Melissa's story encourage you to keep moving in the direction of your dreams. Let it inspire you to go forward and make your next days your best days.

No More Excuses

Take a moment to identify a dream in your life that you haven't gone after because of one reason or another. Write out a few of the excuses you told yourself as to why you couldn't reach the goal. For every excuse you list, create an opposite and positive breakthrough to replace it.

For example, if one dream was to run a half marathon, your excuses could be:

- I don't have enough time.
- It is too far to run.
- I probably wouldn't be able to find a babysitter that day.

In this case, your new breakthroughs would be the following:

- I can and will make the time.
- I will start training by running short distances and building up tolerance and endurance little by little.
- I have several friends who would be happy to watch the kids so I can achieve my goal!

Remind yourself of these new breakthroughs every day, especially anytime you feel like giving in and giving up. You can do this! Banish the excuses, and you'll be amazed at just how strong you really are.

Dream:

Old Excuses:

New Breakthroughs:

Dream:

Old Excuses:

New Breakthroughs:

PART IV

INCREASING YOUR CAPACITY

One of the definitions of the word *capacity* is "the ability or power to do a task." If you are serious about reaching your dreams and stepping into your Next, then you will have to gain the ability to do the things necessary to reach them. You will have to grow in certain areas of your life and stretch beyond your comfort zone. It can be uncomfortable at times, but wouldn't you trade a little discomfort in the beginning to reach your goal? I know I would!

Chapter 18

YOUR SHIFT
IS A GIFT

t's time to go from neutral to first gear. In other words, it's time to start moving. Sitting idle will get you nowhere.

Learning to drive a standard car can be one of the most challenging and frightening things when you first start. I remember learning to do this when I was a teenager. My first driving lesson was in my brother's car, and I was so nervous when it came time to release the clutch and take off in first gear. I put all my focus and energy into that transition, and once I took off and got going, I wanted to stay in first gear and just cruise through the neighborhood, but that would cause major engine trouble and eventually a breakdown. The problem was that I was too afraid to shift into another gear for fear of stalling out and creating an embarrassing moment. Eventually, over time and with much practice, I was able to shift effortlessly without fear and enjoy the journey.

If you are going to reach your dreams, you must get your shift together. Cruising around in first gear can get you started, but it won't sustain you on the highway to your destiny. If you want more out of life, then it's time for you to gear up for it and make it happen. See this change as a gift—an opportunity for a new beginning.

It's time for you to *shift*!

Shift Your Thinking

The way you thought yesterday has gotten you to where you are today. You must begin to think differently in order to reach your destination tomorrow. Start thinking more positive thoughts about where you are and where you are heading. If you think like a winner, you will act like a winner, so start with thinking better about yourself.

Some people still haven't learned this simple little step, and it has hindered their efforts in reaching their dreams. When you think better thoughts about yourself, then you actually begin to believe in yourself. When you believe in yourself, you have the motivation you need to start moving forward.

> Always remember that you are the first recipient of what-
> ever comes out of your mouth. Take some time to make
> a list of positive and encouraging things you can say to
> yourself on a daily basis. This will result in confidence and
> a boost in your self-esteem.

Shift Your Knowledge

Chances are, your dream requires a new level of knowledge. You will probably have to learn some new techniques, methods, and strategies in order to go from where you are to where you want to be. Don't let this deter you from trying. There is nothing wrong or abnormal about stretching your mind muscle.

I've never really considered myself to be a handyman when it comes to fixing things around the house. After we reached the five-year mark in our new home, it was like one appliance after another began to break or give us issues. The first time a toilet broke, I called the plumber because I didn't even know where to start. The plumber was there for about thirty minutes, and it cost me about $150.

The next thing to go was our icemaker in the refrigerator. I could just hear those dollar signs in my head when I thought about calling the repairman, so I thought I would rely on Google this time to help me out. I looked up "icemaker repair," found some YouTube videos, and tried to investigate the problem on my own.

I did everything the videos were telling me to do but still had no luck with fixing the machine, so I gave up and called the repairman. He walked in and said, "I can see what's wrong with it right now." He showed me how and why the icemaker was broken. It took him *less than one minute* to pinpoint the issue. He was in and out of my house in less than fifteen minutes, replaced a small part, and left with a payment of $280.

Before he arrived, I decided that I would act like his apprentice and learn from him every step of the process. I told myself I will never pay that much again to have something fixed that I can repair or replace myself. Knowledge is power and can save you a lot of money. I'm not a handyman, but I do know how to learn from others.

Shift Your Routine

We talked about this earlier in the book, but it's worth repeating because so many people get stuck right here: don't be insane; it's time to change. Don't be afraid to try something new. You can start out with simple practical things and work your way up.

You might want to start adding some type of daily exercise into your routine. This will definitely switch things up for you, and it will also get your body feeling good and much healthier. You can also find a hobby if you don't already have one; schedule an appointment with your hobby to ensure that you engage in it at least a couple of times a month.

A routine offers too much chance to eventually turn into a rut. You can easily find yourself in a pattern of doing the same thing over and over. Before long you will feel like a hamster on a wheel. You're running and running, but at the end of the day, you are going nowhere. You will feel stuck. When that happens, make a change and keep making changes until you're excited and energized by the new routine.

Shift Your Actions

Dreaming and setting goals is great. Usually when we dream or set goals they pertain to our future. Here's a thought for you—start acting like your future is *now*. Don't wait until you get there; start acting like you are there right now. I've heard it said, "You can act your way into a feeling quicker than you can feel your way into an action." Start acting like you are living your dreams now, and it will cause you to grow into that person more quickly than you realize. Your actions should start moving you in the direction of your dream.

> Take responsibility for where you are.
> Take action for where you want to be.

In a perfect world, it would be so nice to push a button or open an app on your smartphone and presto, you are experiencing the life you dream about. Sorry, it's not that easy. Your dream doesn't happen from the cushy recliner or that comfortable spot on your sofa that has your rear indentation. Your dream turns into reality when you take action and make it happen.

Your life doesn't come with a remote control; if you don't like what you're seeing, then you have to get up, take action, and change it yourself. Yes, it may be hard work but it's well worth it, especially if your actions bring about a greater fulfillment in your life.

Chapter 19

THE POWER OF RIGHT CONNECTIONS

The very first right connection that I know I made in my life came when I was seventeen years old. I was in my senior year of high school, and my parents had just gone through a terrible divorce that left me without a father figure in my life. I was a little lost and confused about what I was going to do with my life after high school.

My mother attended church and made me go as well. I was reluctant at first, but then something happened. The youth pastor, Bill Moore, saw me one day as I was walking out of church, and he made a statement I still vividly remember. He pointed at me and said, "There goes that mighty young man of God." That's all he said, but from that day forward, he was the first connection that led me to many more right and strategic connections in my life, no doubt taking me from where I was to where I wanted to be. He remains a mentor and friend to this day.

Connecting with the right person is vital for you. The right person is able to bring out the best in you and even prepare you to do things that you thought were way beyond your current skill set. They can introduce you to new ideas and spark so much creativity in you that you didn't even know existed. Simply put:

making right connections will always take you to the next level.

Everyone needs a coach or a mentor in his or her journey of life. Warren Sapp is a former NFL football defensive tackle and also a Hall of Famer. When he was being inducted into the Hall of Fame, he was asked what factors contributed to his getting such a prestigious honor. He talked about his relationship with one of the NFL's greatest coaches, Tony Dungy. He said that Coach Dungy would mail him a handwritten letter before every training camp, telling him what the next step was for him to be great and make a difference. Warren Sapp said those letters were his motivation and he looked forward to them every season.

> Anytime you see a turtle up on top of a fence post,
> you know he had some help. —Alex Haley

Kung Fu Connections

I'm sure you remember the classic movie *The Karate Kid*, starring Ralph Macchio, who played Daniel, a teenager faced with bullying, and Pat Morita, who played Mr. Miyagi, a janitor at Daniel's apartment complex. Daniel finds himself being singled out, bullied, and picked on by a group of guys at school. When he retaliates, he quickly finds out that these teenagers are all skilled in karate. One night they chase Daniel all the way back home and begin beating him up. Mr. Miyagi comes out of nowhere and saves the day by warding off Daniel's attackers quickly and swiftly.

Later on, Daniel, in an effort to eventually strike back once and for all, tries to convince Mr. Miyagi to teach him the art of self-defense so that he can fight fire with fire and repay those bullies. Mr. Miyagi has a different viewpoint on the art of self-defense and sees it as a way of doing good versus using it for brutality. With much pleading from Daniel, Mr. Miyagi finally agrees to show Daniel how to defend himself through the art of karate.

Now this is where it gets interesting. Daniel's expectation of being taught karate is much different than Mr. Miyagi's teaching techniques. To Daniel's surprise and disappointment, his training consists of doing the following chores for Mr. Miyagi:

- Painting the house and fence.
- Washing and waxing the cars.
- Sanding the floor of his outside deck.

Daniel, although he doesn't quite understand this, reluctantly does each chore with the expectation that Mr. Miyagi will eventually show him the real techniques once he finishes the chore. As time goes on, Daniel feels like Mr. Miyagi's personal slave and is ready to throw in the towel and quit. In a famous scene where Daniel confronts Mr. Miyagi after finishing a long night of doing chores, Mr. Miyagi, fully confident in his selection of training methods, asks Daniel to show him the karate from the chores that he had done throughout the week. Brilliance explodes in the scene as Daniel uses all of those movements from doing chores to fend off the punches and kicks from Mr. Miyagi.

Daniel began to assume that Mr. Miyagi was the wrong person for the job, when he was no doubt the right person and the right connection that Daniel needed in order to accomplish his goal. Just like the connection between those two characters, there's a person out there who can influence you in a way that will unleash your inner karate kid!

No dream or goal can be accomplished alone. If it can, then it's not much of a dream at all. Connecting with the right people is vital to the success of your dream. There is always someone out there who has been where you are now, and they are willing to share a plethora of tips and action steps that will get you to your Next. They have been through the ups and downs, setbacks, and moments when they felt like giving up. They can be a great resource for you while you are in the process of going from where you are to where you want to be.

This means it's time for you to start looking for those people who are living the life you want to live. This doesn't mean for you to idolize them or even want to be like them. It simply means recognizing that they are a source of knowledge and wisdom. You can't look at it like you are only using them to get where you want to be. Trust me, the majority of successful people love sharing their story with others.

Their success story, tips, instruction, or opinions usually comes in different forms. Today's world of social media and technology has made it possible for people to share life-changing information with the click of a button.

Social Media Searching

When I began to feel a change coming in my current position in life, I had a strong desire to enhance my blogging, write books, and do more public speaking. By that time, I had already started a blog and already did my fair share of public speaking. Still, I had a strong desire to take both of those to another level.

Writing a book was going to be a new experience since I had never written a book before and was clueless about the process and all the details it took to actually publish a book. The next step for me was to find people who were already doing those things, such as writing and blogging, and learn from them. It didn't mean that I was going to have a personal relationship with or even meet them, but I knew I had to start somewhere.

I started following certain people on Twitter and social media who were in the arena where I knew I was headed. Some of them were successful bloggers and authors who shared limitless resources on their websites and blogs, which included instructional videos, how-tos, and even the step-by-step procedure of writing and publishing your own book.

There are hundreds, if not thousands, of knowledgeable people for you to connect with via social media. You can start right now by subscribing to their blog or newsletter, reading their books, and listening to their podcasts. Remember: free knowledge is only valuable when you put it to use; otherwise it just lies around waiting for the next man or woman to get it and actually do something with it.

Another thing I did was join a life group at my church that was geared toward helping those who had a desire to write a book. It was a perfect fit for me and perfect timing as well. The group was led by two ladies from my church, each with a background in this field. One was an editor who worked for large publishing companies, and the other was an author of several books. They both knew the ins and outs of how to publish a book. Each week, they would invite a guest speaker from the book business to give us pointers, tips, knowledge, and ideas.

Take Action to Connect

Make a list of at least three to five people you can connect with immediately to receive a download of valuable information in the arena that you are leaning toward. Remember, these don't have to be people in close proximity of you. Social media is filled with people who are sharing free information every day through social media platforms and personal blogs. If you don't know who to connect with, ask some of your family members, friends, or coworkers, and you will likely get some great suggestions.

Five people you should connect with:

1.

2.

3.

4.

5.

Now, making the list is only half the task. You need to follow through and actually make some sort of connection with the people that you just identified, whether in person, through email, through their blog, or by following them on social media.

Get Uncomfortable

We're not all extroverts with outgoing personalities who love talking to strangers. But being an introvert is no excuse for not meeting new people. In order to connect with the right people, you will have to step outside your comfort zone. As proof, here's a quick story about connecting with new people.

As an introvert, I sometimes find it a task or even awkward to meet new people. However, over the years I've learned it is vital to make new connections because they have the potential to lead to great opportunities and open doors that I never would have found on my own. Because I know that, I've pushed myself to get outside my comfort zone.

One day I stopped off at Starbucks to do a little writing and social media work before going to church. I went up to the counter and placed my order, and as I was walking away, a gentleman was standing there waiting on his coffee and said, "Hello," and commented that I looked familiar to him. Now, being a pastor, I run into people all over Nashville who know me and come up to me. Sometimes I feel like I'm wearing one of those name badge stickers—but I don't always recognize them in return! So my immediate response was, "Hey, how've you been?"

For a moment I thought to myself, "I don't have time to talk because I need to work on a few projects and then head to church." But I did the right thing and engaged in conversation. I told him I was a pastor, and when we realized we didn't really know each other after all, I suggested that maybe he'd visited our church at one time and that's why I looked familiar. There was a little small talk about me, and then I asked him what he did. He told me he was the publisher of a couple of magazines, and I immediately realized that perhaps this was a connection I was supposed to make.

I gave him my card, we talked about the dating book that Heather and I had just released, and that was that. He seemed intrigued as I described the book and agreed it was a much-needed topic. The whole conversation took about five minutes, but there's no telling what could come of it in the future.

If you are ever going to reach your Next, you are going to have to make new connections. It's not that you are ungrateful for the old connections that you already have. Those connections are great and have gotten you to where you are now. But in order for you to go from where you are to where you want to be, you must set your expectations on the next connections. And for those of you who need a little extra help (I would be one of those people too), here are a few ways to make new connections:

Don't be consumed with your agenda.

Be aware of the fact that there are other people all around you that are in search of their next connection. Be willing to engage in conversation with a total stranger and see what could happen. It's okay to be focused on your task, but be ready to make an allowance for an unexpected interruption that could lead to a great connection. You just never know who is sitting in that coffee shop with you. The person at your table at the networking luncheon just might be the right connection to take you to your next level.

Be prepared.

If you're like me, you have the tendency to forget people's names (though I'm working on that). Always have your business card on you. If all else fails, at least have a website that you can give them to quickly point to you and your information. My new friend didn't have his card on him that day, but I gave him mine and briefly told him the navigation steps to get to my new book page from my website. Another great idea is to scribble a few notes on the business card you receive from someone else so you'll remember the conversation you had.

Here's a quick tip: When I know I'm going to be at a coffee shop working or meeting someone, I make it a practice to always have a conversational piece, like one of my books or my business card, on the table for people to see as they walk by. I can't tell you how many times someone has walked by and been intrigued enough to ask a few questions, which has led to a brief conversation and the handing out of my business card.

Follow up.

If you make a new connection, it's important to follow up immediately. If you put it at the end of your to-do list, you will probably never get to it. If you walk away with their business card, email, or social media platforms, then make it a rule to quickly send them a note, direct message, or tweet that simply says something like, "It was great meeting you today at Starbucks. Good luck with the magazines you are publishing. Send me a link, I would love to check them out."

The man I met at Starbucks followed up with me minutes after he left Starbucks that day. He sent me an email and expressed interest in my book, gave me his contact information, and indicated that he'd like to stay in touch. And you know what? To this day we stay in touch with each other via social media and have even had a coffee meeting since then. You just never know what the next connection will bring about for you. It just might get you to your next level.

Everyone Needs Encouragement

It's important to intentionally connect with people who will encourage you along the journey. They don't have to have any experience in the next thing for your life, but they can be that voice of inspiration and motivation that causes you to stay the course. At the end of the day, encouragement goes a long, long way. To illustrate this fact, here's the story of a great example of this kind of person.

One day I ran a 5K with my good friend, Antjuan. He's an avid runner like I am, and we were both excited to be running together. This particular race was at a local farm and had a few obstacles (fence climbing, jumping over bales of hay, etc.) along the way. As we were running, I was reflecting on just how important it is to have a good running buddy with you since we are all in a race and headed somewhere.

As the race went on, it got harder and harder; but Antjuan didn't let me quit. In fact, here are three ways Antjaun kept me running that day:

1. He communicated his support and commitment up front.

Right before we started the race, he looked at me and said, "Now, Adonis, you invited me and I'm your guest and I am here to run at your pace. If you want to go faster, I'll go faster, and if you want to slow down, I'll slow down." As I thought about that statement, it became clear to me that we can get so focused on our own race that we forget to support others on their race. The quickest way to finish your race is to help someone else finish theirs.

2. He checked on me periodically throughout the race.

Throughout the entire race, we ran side by side. At different stages of the race, he would ask me how I was doing. This is so easy to do, but oftentimes we forget to check on others in their race. Make it a point to reach out to your friends and family. A simple "How are you doing?" goes a long, long way and makes a huge difference to the recipient.

3. He encouraged me the whole time.

He kept saying things like, "We got this," "We're doing good," "This is a good pace," and finally, "We're almost to the finish line!" His encouragement was over the top, and I was extremely thankful for it.

I also realized that even though it was so natural and easy for him, this is something that any of us can do, regardless of how outgoing we are. If there's one thing I know about people, it's that we all need encouragement at one time or another.

There was absolutely no way I would have finished that race at a decent time without Antjuan. There were numerous times when his voice counteracted the voice in my head that was telling me to quit or slow down. Antjuan was definitely providing a great source of encouragement and motivation for me that day.

I learned that it is of high importance for everyone to have this kind of person in their life if they are on a journey to their Next. Also keep in mind the karma factor: what goes around comes around. Try helping someone else reach his or her goal, and you'll see how in return someone will help you reach yours.

Antjuan is a great leader because he always wants to help others reach their goals and accomplish their dreams. That is what a good running buddy does, and that is what a good encourager does. So go and do likewise.

Run the Race with Someone Today

Remember that while you are on the journey to your Next, there are others on the journey to theirs who need encouragement as well. Make it a daily or weekly habit to intentionally encourage someone in your sphere of influence.

Here are a few practical ways to offer encouragement:

- Send a text message.
- Post a nice message on a social media page.
- Send an email.
- Send a handwritten letter.
- Make a phone call.

Chapter 20

LETTING GO OF
TRADITIONS

Sometimes it's so easy to get stuck in life simply because we've been doing life one way for so long that we are not open to anything new. In reality, a new way of doing things can open up a whole new world for you and allow you to move out of Settleville.

As the times continue to change and shift, and with technology exploding in leaps and bounds, you will have to let go of some of your old ways of doing and thinking if you are ever going to reach your next level in life. Yes, your current ways of working, thinking, and acting may create success, but as time goes on, the same routines may not work.

Tradition is frozen success. —Dr. Myles Munroe

Have you ever heard the story of the Christmas ham? A young lady was preparing a ham one day while her friend was visiting. She cut the end off of the ham before placing it in the pan to bake. When her friend asked why she cut the end off the ham before putting it into the oven, the young lady replied, "I really don't know why, but I've always seen my mother do that."

Several days later, the young lady was talking with her mother and remembered that her friend had asked her about the ham. The young lady asked her mother why she always cut the end off the ham before baking it. Her mother said, "I'm not sure why, but that's the way Mom would always do it."

A few weeks later, the young lady went to visit her grandmother. While there, she remembered her conversation with her mom about the ham, and she asked her grandmother why she cut the end off the ham. Her grandmother replied, "Well dear, if I didn't cut the end off, it would have never fit into my baking pan."

Three generations down the line, a tradition was being carried out that was no longer needed. It worked in its day because a shorter pan was all the grandmother had to work with. But that tradition failed to change over time. It's a cute story and a good reminder that we should question traditions we know nothing about. You would be amazed at how many people continue to do things a certain way just because that's the way that their parents or grandparents did it, and now they have been doing it that way for years as well.

Question Your Habits

The definition of the word *tradition* is "a long-established or inherited way of thinking or acting." You can also often interchange the word *tradition* with the word *habit*, which means "a settled or regular tendency or practice, especially one that is hard to give up."

Now I'm not saying that all traditions or habits are bad and that you need to get rid of every one of them. What I am saying is that maybe it's time to ask yourself the important questions regarding those habits.

- Why am I not moving forward?
- Why do I always give up?
- Why haven't I gone in the direction of my dreams?
- Why do I always give excuses as to why I can't do something?
- Why do I always think this way?
- Why do I always respond to difficult times this way?

You need to be able to identify those traditions and habits that you have received as hand-me-down traditions or those habits that you have started on your own that are no longer needed. These very well could be the mind-sets and actions that are holding you back from reaching your Next.

It's time to let them go and move forward. Think of it this way: you don't have to cut the end off the ham anymore.

Chapter 21

EMBRACING CHANGE

Have you ever found yourself in a place where you are not happy with the way your life is going? If where you are is not where you want to be, then don't fear change—embrace it.

Accept it and everything changes; reject it and nothing happens. If you're stuck in your life, then rejecting change can only give you the same of what you already don't enjoy. I'm not talking about changing the color of your hair or your eyes or replacing your wardrobe with the latest fashion. I'm talking about that change that will make a difference in your life and help you get to your next level.

Remember, your life doesn't get better by chance; it gets better by change.

> Nothing happens until the pain of remaining
> the same outweighs the pain of change. —Arthur Burt

I like to do a lot of my writing at my neighborhood coffee shop. It's a great environment with lots of wonderful people from my community. On the counter by the register sits a tip jar. The slogan on it, although creative, is also very thought provoking. The sign on the tip jar says, "If you fear change, leave it here."

Research has shown that a large percentage of the world's population fears or hates change. I used to be one of those included in that percentage. I used to *hate* change. It bothered me so much because it had the potential to disrupt my life and mess up my already set and proven routine.

The farther I've gone in my journey, the more I realize that I need change to reach my destination. I've learned to welcome change and even create change in areas of my life. I now understand that there is great power in the ability to make and adapt to change.

You can't expect great things to happen without expecting great change to take place.

> Change isn't always bad.
> Sometimes change is good. Sometimes it shows
> you where you were meant to be all along. —*Shey Stahl*

Four Simple Changes That Can Make Your Life Better

1. Change your thinking.

Your thoughts are powerful instruments that can move you toward your dreams and goals in life. Thoughts can also discourage you if you are thinking negative things about your future. Instead of thinking you can't do something, start thinking you can! Let positive thoughts about your future dominate your mind. Start thinking like a champion and see yourself being the best at whatever it is you desire to do. Instead of thinking about all the things that could go wrong, start thinking about all the things that could go right when you start moving toward your Next.

You must change from negative thinking to positive. Some people never get to the point of taking action because they scare themselves away. Their thoughts are so negative when it comes to going after their dreams that they simply never make an attempt to achieve them. Their negative thinking stops them dead in their tracks every time.

Here are a few examples of what I call "Negative 'What if' Thinking":

- What if I step out in faith and fail?
- What if I crash and burn and look like a fool?
- What if I can't finish what I start?
- What if I'm not good enough to do this?
- What if I don't have what it takes to be successful?

This kind of negative thinking will never get you anywhere. It will drain you and exhaust you to the point of never trying to reach for your dreams.

Now, here are a few examples of what I call "Positive 'What If' Thinking":

- What if I take a step of faith and everything works out fine?
- What if I don't let the opinions of others stop me?
- What if I believe that failure will compel me to keep pushing?
- What if I look fear in the face and still keep moving forward?
- What if I believe in myself like never before?
- What if I reach for my Next and get there?

It takes the same amount of energy to think a negative thought as it does to think a positive thought. The only thing that influences the outcome is which one you believe.

2. Change your self-talk.

You are the first recipient of whatever comes out of your mouth. If you are speaking negatively about yourself and your future, then you will no doubt manifest what you say.

We can be our worst enemy by saying the wrong things to ourselves. It's time for the "now you" to start talking like the "future you." Start talking like a successful person right now. Let your language be powerful, inspiring, and motivating.

> I am the greatest,
> I said that even before I knew I was.
> —Muhammad Ali

You must always remember that you have the ability to be your greatest encourager. Trust me, on the journey to your Next you will definitely come across detours, roadblocks, and setbacks. You will experience exciting times as well as depressing times. It's in those moments when discouragement tries to settle in that you will need to speak positive things to yourself like never before. Do whatever you have to do to get yourself energized and encouraged.

- Put sticky notes on your bathroom mirror with encouraging and motivating quotes so you can say them on a daily basis.
- Create a playlist compiled of your favorite speakers and listen to them while driving to work.
- Go to a comedy show. You may not know this, but laughter is good for the heart, soul, and mind.

Think of this compilation of encouraging notes, helpful material, and stress-relieving activities as your Emotional Maintenance

Program. You see, while you're on this journey to your Next, your emotions will feel as if they are on a roller coaster at times—up and down, loop to loop, and all of the above will drive your emotions to many different places. An Emotional Maintenance Program will serve as a safeguard and will already be in place to help stabilize your emotions when they get out of line.

> Take the time right now to write out at least three action steps that will be a part of your Emotional Maintenance Program:
>
> 1.
>
> 2.
>
> 3.

What you say to yourself, about yourself, matters most. Here are a few of the statements I often say to myself:

- It's not over.
- I may be down, but I'm not out.
- Today I will bounce back.
- Today I am only stronger because of yesterday.
- I'm still alive.
- I got this no matter what.
- I will get back up.
- I will not quit.
- My worst days are behind me.
- The best is yet to come.
- Today I will reach my dreams.

- Today I will accomplish my goals.
- Today I will win.
- Today I will make it.
- Today I will overcome.
- Today I will do the impossible.
- Nothing will stop me.
- I am ready, aimed, and focused.
- I am fearless, bold, confident, and courageous.
- I am strong, tough, and resilient.
- I am victorious!

3. Change your expectation.

It's time to start enlarging your expectation. Don't let your circumstances determine your expectations. You should wake up every morning expecting that you're going to have a great day, regardless of how you feel.

Expect opportunities to meet you today. Expect good fortune to come your way. Expect that whatever you set out to do will be accomplished. See yourself living the life that you have imagined. If you can't see it, then you will never be it.

> Most people never achieve anything
> because they simply don't expect to.

I briefly mentioned in an earlier chapter that there was a time in my life when I worked as a carpet cleaner. I needed a job at the time, and it helped pay my bills. Just because it wasn't my dream job didn't meant that I didn't give it 100 percent. It wasn't long before they made me a crew chief, and every day I would have a different assistant with me on the truck.

One of the things I noticed among some of the workers was that they had a negative expectation even before they got into the customer's house. It's no secret that a carpet-cleaning company, just like many other companies that provide a service to you, will ask you to purchase more of their products on the spot in addition to what you already agreed to. Many of the workers would say things like, "Customers don't want anything extra," or "I'll never sell anything on this route today."

But I had come to realize that the key was all in a positive expectation, much like my friend who worked at the mall kiosk. I began to tell my assistants, "Today we are going to have a great day. We are going to have great customers who will be so excited about the work that we do that they will want to pay for other things in addition and will also leave us a good tip for lunch." It didn't happen all the time, but it happened more than enough that I ended up having the kind of day that I expected—so much that many of my customers would refer me to their friends and family, and that created great repeat business for the company and me.

Now remember, I said having a positive expectation was the key, not a magic wand. Nothing just magically happens, but a positive expectation will be the key to open up many doors of opportunity that you didn't even know were out there.

4. Change your attitude.

Great opportunity is seldom seen through the lens of a bad attitude. What I mean by this is that a bad attitude causes you to create a negative outcome in your mind when an opportunity presents itself. Therefore, your attitude will either cause you to see the opportunity and pursue it, or let it go on to the next person.

A positive attitude will take you far in life. When people have a bad, negative attitude, it is usually because they are not satisfied with their current circumstance or situation in life. A bad attitude never changed anything. Choose to be positive today and have a great attitude, no matter what comes your way. Like a virus, attitudes are contagious. Your positive attitude will produce great results for you and others around you.

> Your attitude determines your altitude.
> —Zig Ziglar

Make sure that you are aware of your attitude every day. Keep a good pulse on it, and when you notice it's taking a dive, that's the time to revisit your Emotional Maintenance Program.

Chapter 22

KISS MEDIOCRITY GOODBYE

One of the saddest, most depressing times in a person's life is often when they know they have settled in life, and they know they could have done more with their talents, energy, potential, and time than what they have done. They regret not pushing themselves further. They regret not doing more of what they were capable of doing.

- Mediocrity doesn't challenge you.
- Mediocrity doesn't motivate you.
- Mediocrity doesn't stretch you.
- Mediocrity doesn't push you.

If you are honest with yourself, it doesn't take a big revelation to know when you are camping out in mediocrity. Most people already know when they are doing just enough to get by at work, school, or home. The tendency is to give less than 100 percent in their efforts, knowing that their minimized efforts still maintain a sufficient flow of producing what's required of them. They have no desire to push themselves beyond their limits. They have settled into a place of comfort and ease.

Let me tell you, my friend, comfort and ease will never pave the way to your destiny. If you are ever going to reach your Next, then you can't camp out in the woods of mediocrity any longer. It's time for you to push yourself beyond the place of doing just enough. There is more in you, and you know it. It's time to unleash it and watch yourself go beyond your limits and into your greatness.

Things really begin to happen and change takes place whenever we go beyond our normal status quo. Quit allowing yourself to nestle safely and comfortably in the lap of mediocrity. Start today by pushing yourself further than you thought you could ever go. Dig down deep and give it your all—and then some. Quit doing just enough to get by at your current job, at your school, or in your marriage. You are better than that. You have what it takes. Allow yourself to step into an environment that draws out the Rocky Balboa in you, and you will surprise yourself by going the distance.

Set New Goals

Several years ago, my wife and I set some health goals for ourselves. As we were planning to have children, we knew that we wanted to be around for a long time to enjoy them and keep up with them. A lady in our church, Shellie Cimarosti, held TaeBo classes with her husband, Mark. We had heard of TaeBo, and I had even tried a TaeBo DVD one time, but I never made it past the warm-up routine because I was too exhausted.

Shellie kept inviting both of us to her class, but we let excuses get in the way. Did I mention that Shellie is the daughter of Billy Blanks, the founder of TaeBo? She is one of the best TaeBo instructors out there—and we were looking for someone who would probably take it easy on us. The truth was the thought of that type of workout for an hour scared us to death! We weren't sure we could do it, and we didn't want to pass out in the middle of the class and embarrass ourselves in front of everyone.

So we remained content with our evening walks and occasionally a light jog through our neighborhood for about three months. Our choice of activity wasn't pushing us at all. We were too comfortable with it. It wasn't getting us anywhere near our weight or health goals, and we were only fooling ourselves by thinking that we were doing enough. The truth was that we were doing just enough to get by—we were simply maintaining our current fitness levels, which would not get us to our individual goals.

This is where you have to be honest with yourself. You know if you are doing just enough to get by. If that's you, then don't beat yourself up over it—go out and change it, starting right now. Get ready to push!

Shellie kept reaching out to us and inviting us to come; she even told us there would be daycare available to take away any excuses we might have for not coming to class. After months of her gentle persistence, we finally agreed to visit a class.

The decision to actually go to a class was the easiest thing about the whole endeavor. The actual class was exactly what we expected. It kicked our butts! We were exhausted to the point of almost throwing up. I remember having to walk out for fear of passing out. But the reality was that this was *exactly* what we needed to push ourselves beyond the point of just getting by.

When we finished the workout, I sat there on the floor in a puddle of sweat realizing I had just kissed mediocrity goodbye. I knew that if I wanted to keep getting closer to my goal, I would have to suck it up and push myself to go to the next TaeBo class. After each class, we were exhausted, but we also felt better. We also felt a sense of accomplishment. We knew we had entered a zone beyond our normal comfort levels. And we began to see results after about two months of attending the weekly class.

The more we kept going, the more we pushed ourselves each time. In fact, we actually looked forward to classes because we knew how great we would feel after we finished!

There is no greater feeling than pushing yourself beyond your comfort zone, knowing that you have given it everything that you've got. You are paving the way for your Next. Keep going, keep pushing, and by all means keep kissing mediocrity goodbye.

I'm so glad Shellie was persistent, because if she hadn't been, then we probably never would have taken a step in that direction. We all need those people in our lives to help push us in the right direction to go beyond our status quo.

> I firmly believe that any man's finest hour,
> the greatest fulfillment of all that he holds dear,
> is that moment when he has worked his heart out
> in a good cause and lies exhausted on the field
> of battle—victorious. —Vince Lombardi

Move Over, Mediocrity!

With complete honesty, take a look over all the areas of your current stage of life and identify where mediocrity is present. You know what they are; you don't need a rocket scientist to point them out for you. You already know when you are doing just enough to get by in a certain area of your life. Start by writing out three or four areas. Once you have made the list, begin to think of ways you can get out of the mud of mediocrity that is only slowing you down. Challenge yourself in each one of these areas to do more and give it 100 percent. You might even need to write out some simple action steps you can take to ensure that mediocrity goes away in those areas of your life.

Area of Mediocrity:

How I Will Kiss It Goodbye:

Area of Mediocrity:

How I Will Kiss It Goodbye:

Chapter 23

PREVAILING WITH PATIENCE

W henever my grandmother taught me a lesson about patience, she would always say, "Baby, sometimes the long way home is the quickest route." Years later I was finally able to understand the meaning behind the wisdom she instilled in me. I believe that patience is not only a virtue but also a key to developing character, endurance, and perseverance that eventually leads us to a place of success.

> The key to everything is patience. You get the chicken by hatching the egg, not by smashing it. —Arnold Glasgow

In today's society it's so easy to look at the success of others and somehow think that they got there overnight without any setbacks or shortcomings. We then have the tendency to look at ourselves and feel that we are behind in our journey and time is running out. This type of thinking only causes us to go into a warp-speed mode, cut corners, and ultimately skip a lot of important learning lessons and steps in the journey.

I believe time spent on the journey will pay off in the end. I've never met a successful person who said, "I wish I would have gotten here sooner." However, I have met successful people who will spend hours telling you about the length of their journey and all the lessons they learned along the way.

Patience Takes Practice

Let's face it: some of us are still dealing with that old childhood mentality of "I want it now." This got us nowhere as children, and it will get us nowhere as adults. If you lack patience, then it's time for you to start mastering the art of patience in your life. Learn to be patient in the small practical things first:

- Not opening the microwave door until the time has completely run out.
- Not passing a slower driver only to beat them to the red light.
- Not putting up your Christmas decorations until after Thanksgiving.
- Be the last one off the airplane on your next flight, no matter where your seat is located.

Some of these examples seem easy to do, but in fact they are very hard for some people to do, including myself. However, this will teach you not to rush the process and get too far ahead of yourself. When you rush the process, you run the risk of a potential failure, all because you didn't have the patience to wait a little bit. You are trying to make things happen instead of allowing things to happen. Believe me, there is a big difference between the two.

Patience is a sign of maturity. Impatient people have a tendency to get angry or irritable when they feel like something is taking too long. This causes a person to try and make something happen more quickly than it was supposed to happen. Let's face it, when you are impatient, it causes a plethora of different emotions to run through your mind, none of which are usually good.

Resist the Warp-Speed Mentality

Success doesn't happen overnight. Rome was not built in a day, and it took your mother nine months to make you. Things worth having are worth waiting for. Slow and steady steps can often get you to the finish line the fastest way.

Everyone remembers the childhood story of *The Tortoise and the Hare*. A bragging, speedy hare challenges a slow-moving tortoise to a race. The tortoise accepts the challenge, and the race begins. The hare is so conceited that he figures he can stop and take a nap because the tortoise is so slow. Unfortunately for the hare, he oversleeps while the slow-moving tortoise consistently advances toward the finish line. The hare wakes up, but it's too late, and the tortoise is crowned the winner! At the end, the tortoise looks at the hare and says, "Slow and steady does it every time."

One of my Bible school instructors shared a particular saying with a group of us eager Bible school students that were ready to conquer the world. He simply said, "Slow growth is good growth." He then took us outside for a visual object lesson.

The school was located on 553 acres of land and had many large oak trees. He walked up to an oak tree with mushrooms all around its base. He looked at the mushrooms and told us that they practically sprung up over the course of one or two days. He then kicked over several of the mushrooms without much effort at all. Then he looked at the oak tree and said, "This oak tree has been growing slow and steady for many years. Now who wants to kick it over?"

Let's face it. We live in a speed-driven society. We speed read. We drive fast. We want a fast-track diet so we can lose weight overnight, and of course, we won't settle for anything less than high-speed Internet connectivity. Keep in mind, while living in a warp-speed world, it's okay to switch gears, slow your pace, and still enjoy great rewards. Remember that your life is not a sprint, it's a marathon—slow and steady does it every time!

He that can have patience can have what he will.

—Benjamin Franklin

Practicing Patience

Here's a great exercise you can do to become more patient. Whenever you find yourself in an impatient mood and all kinds of emotions are running through your mind, *stop* and do this two-minute drill.

1. Recognize that you are feeling impatient.
2. Set a two-minute alarm on your phone, watch, computer, etc.
3. Be still for those entire two minutes and do absolutely *nothing*.

This is not a waste of your time as you might initially think, especially if you're impatient! This is putting patience into practice. The key is to clear your mind, relax, and just be at ease. Feel free to adjust the time limit as needed. Let your emotions settle before resuming whatever you were previously doing.

Chapter 24

LEARN TO TAKE
THE LEAP OF FAITH

S ome people spend their lives standing on the edge of "I will when the timing is right" instead of taking the leap of faith and trusting that things will work out. Here's a great story about my friend Ted Bradshaw and his journey into his Next. It's an amazing yet simple story and can become anyone's reality if they set their minds to it.

When Ted and his wife, Charity, moved to Nashville from Texas, Ted decided that he was going to go to a temp agency and look for a warehouse job. He wanted a nine-to-five job that would allow him to be home every night with his wife.

Everything happened just as Ted planned, and he started an eight-year tenure at a warehouse as an assistant manager. For the first five years at the warehouse, everything went great for Ted. He knew he was right where he was supposed to be, and the job even brought fulfillment beyond just doing his work responsibilities. Ted was a Christian and had a passion and a desire to help others in their Christian walk and faith, so he started a Bible study at the warehouse during lunch breaks for any of the employees who wanted to attend. Life was great for Ted and his family during those years.

Somewhere around year six at the warehouse, things began to change. Ted started feeling like there was something more for him somewhere else. The employees who had come to his Bible study moved on to other jobs, and Ted found himself beginning to settle in to an everyday routine of being the assistant manager. He began to wonder what the next thing was for his life. With a growing family and an increased cost of living, Ted's wife, Charity, started a beauty salon in her home as a way to bring in extra income.

During that time, the warehouse had several head managers come through the company, but none of them stayed long term. One of the new managers even stated that he wasn't going to stay long because he had plans of joining the military.

Ted was doing inventory for the warehouse and was doing a great job of it. At the same time, he kept seeing different managers come and go and thought perhaps his company would give him an opportunity to apply for the head manager position. It made perfect sense to Ted, especially since he had been there for several years and part of his responsibilities were to help train the newly hired head managers.

Yet when Ted went to his boss and inquired about the head manager position, he was told that he couldn't get the job because he didn't have a college degree. They loved his work and expressed how valuable he was to the company, but because he lacked the college degree, he wasn't eligible for the position.

> Sometimes when you're feeling stuck you
> have a sense that you will take any other job offer
> just to escape where you are. —Ted Bradshaw

This left Ted devastated. He felt as if the company had no faith in him, even though he was already doing a great job there. Pretty soon, with no chance of advancement, he started feeling stuck and knew he needed to do something about it. He'd come home every day with an unsettled feeling in the pit of his stomach that just wouldn't leave him alone. So for the first time in years, Ted started contemplating the idea of going back to school and getting a degree. All of his life he thought that if you didn't have the money for college, you just couldn't go. Ted knew that if he went back to school, it would mean huge sacrifices for him and his entire family. He also knew that if he went through all the trouble to go back to school, it was going to be for something other than being a manager at the warehouse.

He read a book entitled *Forty-Eight Days to the Work You Love*. Then he sat down and tried to identify the areas that he was passionate about and the things he wanted to get out of a new career. He narrowed down his focus to three things:

- He knew he wanted to help people.
- He knew he wanted his time to be flexible.
- He knew he needed something that would bring a greater level of income.

Out of that, Ted came up with several career paths to take into consideration. Two of the career paths were to be a pastor or to be a nurse. When Ted was in high school his sophomore year, he broke his back in a bad car accident. He also tore his spleen and intestines and was in pretty bad shape. He remembered that the nursing staff came in and took care of him every day during his stay at the hospital. The nurses made such a huge impact on his life during that time.

Ted finally made a decision and chose nursing as his new career path. He and Charity sat down together and began to look over their budget and all of their options to see if they could even afford for Ted to go back to college. They were in agreement, and Ted knew he couldn't do it without Charity's support. Because of their strong faith and belief in God, they prayed for direction and for an answer. They knew it would take a miracle and a huge leap of faith on their part.

Sometimes you just have to take the leap
and build your wings on the way down. —Kobi Yamada

Ted applied to several schools, but he really wanted to attend Middle Tennessee State University (MTSU). He was accepted at Columbia State instead. His advisor at MTSU recommended that Ted go ahead and attend Columbia State's two-year program and then transfer to MTSU for the remainder of his schooling. They had a bridge program that would provide scholarships and grants that would cover Ted's entire four-plus years of school. The only requirement was that Ted had to make straight As during his first two years at Columbia State in order to qualify for the bridge program.

Now you're probably thinking that's no big deal. I agree; it's probably not a big deal for someone fresh out of high school, but Ted hadn't been in school for more than eighteen years. This was going to be a huge undertaking for him. It meant that he was going to have to put in a lot of hours and hard work to stay at the top of his class. It also meant that the entire family was going to have to make a lot of huge sacrifices in order for all of this to happen.

He told his employers at the warehouse that he was going back to school, but he would be going for a nursing degree instead of going back to qualify for the manager position. The company was fine with that decision, showed their support in the beginning, and even agreed to work with Ted's new college schedule.

Initially he was going to work four ten-hour days, and his company agreed to that arrangement. This would give Ted plenty of time to commit to his new homework schedule. However, two weeks before Ted started college, he was called into the office and told that they had changed their mind and they were no longer going to be able to accommodate the schedule they had agreed on earlier.

This left Ted with a major decision. He knew going back to school was the right thing to do for his life, but he also knew he needed health insurance for his family, which was being provided by his company at the time. At this point he could have let fear stop him in his tracks, but instead he continued with the leap of faith. He left his company and started college.

When he heard that one of the local grocery store chains provided health insurance to part-time employees, he thought it would be perfect and still allow him to focus on school while bringing in an income and providing health insurance for his family. After about two months of working there, he thought it was odd that the human resources department hadn't talked to him about insurance coverage yet. When he talked to them, he got another huge shock—the company had a requirement that part-time employees had to work there for one year before receiving health insurance benefits. So now he was back in the same boat without benefits, and he needed to do something quickly. While Ted was dealing with all of this, he still had to keep up with school-work and his grades. He was under a huge amount of stress.

Ted found himself back on the hunt for a part-time job that offered insurance benefits. His sister-in-law worked for a nation-wide bank that offered full health benefits to part-time employees. Ted explored the opportunity, and this time he was very thorough in his investigation and found out that the benefits would start after thirty days of working there. He applied and got the job. It was a perfect window of opportunity for Ted to work there during his four years of college. Four years later, Ted graduated with honors from MTSU with a bachelor of science in nursing degree. He and his family relocated to Houston, Texas, after graduation to be closer to family, and Ted got a nursing job a few weeks later. This was an answer to their prayers, and they couldn't be happier.

Everything worked out because of Ted's perseverance. He never gave up and never got sidetracked, even though there were many opportunities to do so. Every time he came up against a roadblock, he found another way around it. When I asked Ted what advice he would give others who are searching for their Next, this is what he had to say:

1. Have a clear vision for you, your future, and your family. Have a vision of where you are heading and why you are heading that direction.
2. Get good counsel around you. Have people in your life who can offer you good advice and who are not afraid to tell you the truth.
3. Take action. You can't sit around and expect it to all happen by itself. Your dream is going to take a lot of hard work. If it were easy, then anybody could do it.
4. Count the cost of sacrifice. There will be many sacrifices that you have to be willing to make in order to see your dream become your reality.

5. Perseverance will pay off in the end. There will be plenty of times that you will feel like quitting, but you must dig down deep, push through that feeling, and keep moving forward.
6. Separate yourself from people who will discourage your dream.

No matter what, it's important that you stay committed to your decision and push through the roadblocks and setbacks that you may encounter on the way to your Next. Just like my friend Ted, we all have that inner strength, but some of us just need to learn to tap into it.

No one ever said that it would be easy. If it were easy, then like Ted says, anybody could do it. However, reaching your dream is rewarding when you stick it out and see it through to the end. You will reach a place where you can look back and see that every sacrifice was worth it, and you will be so glad you took the leap to make it happen.

PART V

MAKE YOUR NEXT DAYS YOUR BEST DAYS

Regardless of what has happened in your past, you can turn the tide and start experiencing the best days of your life right now. New opportunities await you. Go after them with everything you've got. The risk will be worth it. You will be so glad that you finally decided to make your dreams a reality.

Chapter 25

GET UP

Have you ever watched a professional fight before? When a fighter gets knocked down to the mat during a match, he has ten seconds to get back up and regain his composure, or he is disqualified and the fight is over. During the time he is on the ground, the referee starts counting. Everyone who is for the fighter that's on the ground begins to shout the words, "Get up!" His trainers, spectators, fans, and even those watching from the comfort of their own homes by television are probably yelling, "Get up!"

When that fighter gets back up, the crowd begins to cheer as he goes on to continue the fight. You see, he was knocked down, but he wasn't out. He overcame that obstacle and showed a resilient spirit that energized everyone around him.

That's how it is when you finally make the decision to go after your dreams. It's like stepping into a boxing ring and contending with all the opposition that is going to come against you. At times you might even feel like you just stepped into the ring with Mike Tyson. A left jab, a right cross, an upper cut, and a bite on the ear—and down you go. The referee starts to count, and you're lying there trying to muster up enough strength to get back up. Maybe you start to wonder if you even want to get back up.

182

> Winners are losers who got up and gave it one more try.
> —Dennis DeYoung

A Knock-Down, Drag-Out Fight

When I was around thirty years old and still living in Texas, I was faced with a very trying time. My finances and food were running out, and there I was, living in a one-bedroom apartment and working at a grocery store to make ends meet. However, the ends were *not meeting*, and I felt like I was going nowhere with my life. I wasn't sure what my next step was or even how I would get to where I wanted to be in life. I still had a dream for more, but it seemed so distant at the time.

I remember the exact day that I literally felt the pressure knock me down to the ground in my little apartment. I had scraped up enough money to go out to eat at a local Chinese buffet. As I sat there eating my meal, the thought of not having enough money to buy groceries for the rest of the week ran through my mind. Fear has a way of making you do some pretty drastic things, and I began to stuff food into my jacket pockets secretly as I sat in my booth, eating alone. I would then go back to the buffet line to fill up another plate, just to return to my seat and stuff some more food into my pockets. I repeated this several times before leaving the restaurant.

When I got back to my apartment and pulled all the food out of my pockets, I realized how desperate my actions were. I thought, "What in the world am I doing? Is this what my future has come to?" The blow of failure knocked me down to my knees, and my future flashed before my eyes. All I saw was a big black empty space, full of nothing.

I sat there on the carpet, crying for what seemed like hours. Thoughts of defeat, failure, and disappointment bombarded my mind. I literally felt the life being sucked right out of me. Then all of a sudden I snapped back to reality. I started believing again. I believed in my faith, and I believed that God still had a plan for my life. I believed in myself and knew I could do this. This was just a temporary circumstance, and if I was strong enough to go the distance, I would eventually see it all change. I believed that I still had a future in spite of my present circumstances.

Like a scene out of a movie, I slowly began to stand back up on my feet right there in my living room—triumphant and strong. As I rose up, I felt my second wind come, and I felt energized to stay in the fight and contend with those negative thoughts that had occupied my mind for those few hours. I felt the weight of failure fall off, and I began to breathe normally again.

That night I came to terms with where I was and where I wanted to be. The next day, I decided to stop the pity party and get back on track with believing in myself and my future. I started dreaming again. I started having faith again. I started speaking positive, encouraging words to myself that energized me to keep moving forward. Ultimately that was a turning point in my life that led me to taking steps in the right direction, and eventually leading to the decision to move to Nashville, Tennessee.

Get Up Again

So many people find themselves going through similar situations. In fact, you may have relived your own scenario in your mind as you read about me stuffing food in my pockets at the buffet.

We have been beat up, beat down, and knocked to the ground

while fighting for our Next. If you have found yourself lying on the ground in the middle of the fight, then right now I want to be your trainer and your greatest fan. Right now I am the one yelling at you, screaming as loud as I can, "Get up! Get up! Get up!"

- Get up from the mat of discouragement that has kept you doubting your future.

- Get up from the mat of disappointment that has drained your energy.

- Get up from the mat of failure that has tried to convince you that you don't have what it takes.

- Get up from the mat of mediocrity that has lulled you into living a lesser life.

- Get up from the mat of fear that has kept you from trying again.

- Get up from the mat of Settleville that has held you captive for years.

- Get up from the mat of humiliation and stop caring what others think about you.

You got this! Get back on your feet and stay in the fight. You are not out, and the fight is not over. It's time to get back on your feet and go the distance.

Trust me, when it's all said and done, you just might be able to borrow that iconic phrase from Rocky Balboa and say for yourself, "Yo, Adrian. I did it!"

Chapter 26

GET READY

Nothing will happen in your future unless you get ready for it. Start taking the necessary action steps to get you ready for what's in store. People who know a certain event is about to happen will usually prepare for it and plan accordingly so the event doesn't catch them off guard.

Rescue workers spend countless hours in training, going through real-life emergency scenarios because they know that one day their skills will be required to help save lives. They prepare so that when that day comes they will be well equipped to handle the situation and they won't be caught off guard. If you're not preparing for your Next, then you're probably not convinced it will take place. If it does happen, you'll be completely unprepared!

The secret of success in life is for a man to be ready for his opportunity when it comes. —Benjamin Disraeli

---

Train Your Brain

A few years ago, I was at Disney World with the family. Every morning I would get up around 6:30 a.m. to go for a run on the jogging trail. On my way to the jogging trail, I would pass the resort pool, where I witnessed the pool staff in their training sessions. One morning I stopped and observed for a while out of curiosity. They went over everything from A to Z. They covered just about every scenario and procedure down to the smallest detail. They did all of this a couple of hours before the pool opened and the guests started arriving for their morning water activities. The lifeguards seemed very confident about their readiness and were extremely focused on looking for any situations that required their assistance. The last thing Disney wanted was for their lifeguards to be unprepared if an opportunity arose.

The last thing you want to do is to be caught off guard or unprepared when your opportunity arises. When you are unprepared, eventually you will drown under the pressure of not being ready to seize the moment.

I think this is a great lesson from Disney and I have incorporated it, to a certain degree, as a strategy when it comes to accomplishing my own personal goals. I think it's important to set aside about thirty minutes each morning to rehearse what you plan to do for the day. You can quickly go over your schedule for the day and play out in your mind the step-by-step actions you will take to produce the desired results. You can even rehearse difficult conversations you might have.

I'm not very fond of meetings, but they are a part of life and if you work within an organization, they are a big part of your weekly responsibilities. Every now and then I have a difficult meeting that I have to attend. The night before the meeting, I rehearse over and over in my mind everything I am going to say during that meeting. Sometimes I go so far as to predict the other person's response so that I can be prepared to respond as well. It creates a better experience for me during the meeting and gives me the confidence to conduct the meeting successfully.

Busting the "Luck" Myth

People who reach their dreams are not lucky; they are hard workers. Luck doesn't have much to do with it at all. In fact, the last thing you want to do is hang your future on luck. One of the greatest golfers of all time, Arnold Palmer, said it best: "The more I practice, the luckier I get." Your success is not based on a roll of the dice; rather, it's based on your level of preparation for the moment. Are you prepared to seize your moment of opportunity when it comes?

> Be ready when opportunity comes…. Luck is when preparation and opportunity meet. —Roy D. Chapin Jr.

Here's a prime example of someone who was prepared. I'm a huge Dallas Cowboys fan, and in November 2014, the Cowboys were playing the New York Giants. In this particular game, Odell Beckham Jr., a wide receiver for the Giants, made what some people believe was undeniably one of the greatest catches in the history of the NFL. He caught a forty-three-yard touchdown pass with one hand—just a few fingers, actually—while in midair, several feet off the ground, and falling backward. (You should Google "Odell Beckham greatest catch" and see it for yourself.) It was truly the most amazing catch that I've seen in football.

The first thing that ran through a lot of people's minds was that he made a lucky catch. The truth of the matter is that Odell Beckham actually spent time practicing catching passes *with one hand*. That's right—he practiced one-handed catches all the time.

Now can you see it? When preparation meets opportunity, great things can happen.

Right now, take advantage of the time that you have to get prepared. Educate yourself about your dream. Start connecting with mentors so you can start learning more about whatever it is that you are passionate about doing. Start creating daily habits that will eventually lead you to tomorrow's success. Gain the education and the knowledge that you need to start moving in the direction of your dreams. Start sharpening your skills and practice, practice, practice!

Chapter 27

GET GOING

Okay, you've been thinking about doing it. You've been dreaming about it. The next thing you need to do is start where you are with what you have. Most people want to start off as an expert, but I'm here to tell you it's perfectly okay to start out as an amateur and work your way up. What's not okay is you never starting at all.

> The start is what stops most people. —Don Shula

Yes, the idea is to dream big and be okay with starting small. Take little steps that will eventually become giant steps along the way. Quit trying to start out at an instant success level. The majority of successful people's "start" no doubt looks different from their ending. Just think about it for a second. The Wright brothers didn't start out with a 747 airplane with jet engines. They started out with a bicycle and some manmade wings! Today millions of people around the world are benefiting from their very small start.

Now it's your turn to take control of your future and make your dream a reality. Don't despise the day of small beginnings. Start now and get ready to make great things happen for you and for others along the way.

You've Thought About It Long Enough

Just thinking about it doesn't really get it done. We can all think of ideas and plans that we've had in the past, and thinking about them was as far as we got in reaching our goal.

Now don't get me wrong, I'm not telling you to skip the think-tank process at all. Yes, you do need to spend some time thinking about the next endeavor or new idea that is rolling around in your head. Thinking about it allows you to plan, strategize, and map out a course of action. The problem is that some people spend way too much time in their think tank. This is largely a result of them wasting time thinking about all the things that *could* go wrong instead of thinking about all the things that *could* go right. They try to think about every single detail and anticipate all the different situations that they will encounter along the way, but that, my friend, is impossible to do from the starting line.

The longer you think about it, the longer it takes for you to take the next step, which is to actually *start doing* what you've been thinking about. Sooner or later, you will have to exit the think tank and enter the field of action.

Just start. That's right—get moving and see what happens. Start doing what you've spent time thinking about. Leave the think tank for a moment and start putting action to those thoughts. Trust me, there will be plenty of times when you will have to get back in your think tank as you keep going in the direction of your dreams.

So the idea of starting now totally makes sense. Think about it—but not for too long.

> The best time to plant a tree was twenty years ago.
> The second best time is now. —Chinese Proverb

It's time for you to make your thoughts become your reality. You can do it.

It's time to quit waiting for everything to line up perfectly. Many people are waiting for all the conditions to be just right or maybe they are waiting for the star constellation to be indicative of their time to start. The time is right now. Five years down the road, you will be so glad that you started *now*.

- Start strategizing a plan of action that will lead you to where you want to be.

- Start making those connections with the right people.

- Start taking those next steps that will move you closer in the direction of reaching the life that you've been dreaming about.

- Start facing those fears head on and move past them. Be determined; push through them no matter the cost.

- Start letting go of yesterday's failures and start embracing tomorrow's possibilities. Put the past behind you and move forward into the new and exciting possibilities for your life.

- Start acquiring the knowledge and skills that it will take to get you where you want to go. The entire world is at your fingertips. Go get it.

Step Away from Stagnation

Make a list of a few ideas or dreams that have been stagnant for some time. List the idea or dream and include the length of time that it has been stagnant. For example, maybe you have dreamed of getting back in shape but haven't been to the gym in more than a year.

Once you make that list, stare at it for a few minutes and realize that the length of time your ideas and dreams have been stagnant will only *increase* if you don't *get going right now*! Then go make it happen!

Chapter 28

QUITTING IS NOT AN OPTION

M ost people are pretty good at starting something, but many have a hard time with the follow-through and actually finishing a project. A lot of people tend to stop when the road gets tough and they start experiencing hardships along the way. Perhaps they had an unrealistic expectation and thought the road would be easy. They also begin to come up with excuses like "I'll get back to it when I have enough time." The real truth is that they will never have *enough* time because they simply won't make time for it anymore.

> If you can't fly, then run, if you can't run, then walk,
> if you can't walk, then crawl, but whatever you do,
> you have to keep moving forward. —Martin Luther King Jr.

It's up to you to break the bad habit of leaving unfinished things lying around. Yes, moving toward your next will require hard work, no matter what it is. Don't make the mistake of thinking that it should be an easy road for you to reach your destiny. In fact, the bigger the dream you have, then the more resistance and adversity you will face on your journey. Some people view opposition to their dream as a sign or indicator that they are going in the wrong direction. They think that it shouldn't be this hard to go from where they are to where they want to be. If you start thinking this way, then no doubt it will be easy for you to give up or stop right in the middle of reaching your Next.

Reasons to Never Give Up

Usually when going after our dreams, goals, and desires, we find ourselves constantly being met with opposition, resistance, and countless doors slammed shut in our face. In reality, many great people have found themselves falling short of their dreams. Failure is not fatal; rather it is a crossroads where we are faced with the option to stop or to keep reaching for success.

I enjoy researching and reading about people of greatness that have gone through failure and still aspired to become some of the most successful and influential people in the world. I've compiled a short list of people who faced failure and yet still took next steps and eventually went on to succeed.

Roger Banister was told it was physically impossible for him to break the three-minute mile. He pressed on and did it anyway. Now today, the three-minute mile is used as a qualifier for some running events. He didn't let the naysayers persuade him to take up residency in Settleville. He stayed focused and was determined to do *the impossible*. He trained for the moment. He prepared for the moment. He kept pushing through disappointments. And don't think for one moment that he accomplished the goal of breaking the three-minute mile the very first time he tried it.

When reading about the story of Roger Banister, you could easily assume that he was able to do it because he was physically fit and had the right genetics and skills to perform such an impossible task. Although he did possess those qualities, I'm sure he was still faced with the thought of giving up a couple times in the middle of this endeavor. But he didn't.

Walt Disney was fired by a newspaper editor because he was told he lacked imagination and had no good ideas. Imagine that, the future creator of imagination beyond belief had no imagination. After that, Disney started a number of businesses that didn't last too long and ended with bankruptcy and failure. Then along came a mouse, and, well, you know the rest of the story.

Chances are you have been to see that magical place called Disney World. That place has been the vacation spot for millions of people and families from all over the world. We go there today and enjoy the fruit of a creative person's labor.

He didn't let his setbacks derail him or cause him to live a lesser life. He kept shaking off the dust of disappointment. His desire to create the life he had been dreaming of was much bigger and grander than the moments of temporary failures. I'm glad he didn't quit. My kids are glad he didn't quit!

Sidney Poitier was told by the casting director at his first audition, "Why don't you stop wasting people's time and go out and become a dishwasher or something?" Poitier vowed to show him that he could make it, going on to win an Oscar and becoming one of the most well-regarded actors in the business. He didn't listen to the negativity of others, and you can't afford to either. If you heed the voice of the critics, they will no doubt slow you down and eventually cause you to come to a stop. Remember, not everyone can see your potential for greatness. Not everyone is going to be on your bandwagon or be your greatest cheerleader.

If Sidney Poitier had listened to the casting director, he never would have done what he did for cinema in his era. His tenacity, resiliency, and fortitude empowered him to break through the race barrier and become one of the first African American actors to take a leading role.

Thomas Edison's teachers told him he was "too stupid to learn anything." He later made one thousand unsuccessful attempts at inventing the light bulb. Of course, all those unsuccessful attempts finally resulted in the design that worked. This is another great story of someone not quitting, even when faced with multiple failures.

This kind of mental strength is only present when you keep your eyes on the prize—the prize of reaching your Next. The prize of accomplishing the goal. The prize of going from where you are to where you want to be. He never took his eyes off of the light bulb that he envisioned in his mind—an invention that would eventually light the world.

I'm sure there were many times he thought of giving up and quitting. There were probably many times when he almost talked himself out of what he was endeavoring to create. But he kept trying … 1,001 times!

So the next time you see a light bulb, don't just take it for granted. Let it be a reminder that someone had to push through many failures in order to produce it.

Go ahead and write your story. Don't have one yet? Then keep at it—it's coming.

Chapter 29

IT'S NEVER
TOO LATE

Too many people buy into the lie that it's too late or that they have missed the boat and it will never come around again. They simply quit trying because they think they are far too old to go after the goals and dreams from their youth. That couldn't be further from the truth. It's not too late now, and it won't be too late a year from now, as long as you still have breath in your body. It's never too late. You always have the choice to start right now, wherever you are, and begin to go after those lifelong dreams.

> It's never too late to start over. If you weren't happy
> with yesterday, try something different today!
> Don't stay stuck. Do better. —Alex Elle

Take my friend Hector, for example. He called me one day and asked if he could take me to lunch because there was something he wanted to share with me. I could sense his excitement and was anticipating our time together. As I sat there listening to him, I knew my friend was about to enter into his Next. He was about take a step in the direction of a dream that he'd had for several years.

Hector was originally from Texas and had been living in Nashville, Tennessee, for the past thirteen years. When he first moved to Nashville, he found a job working as a dispatcher for a rather large nationwide company and had been working there ever since. He was happy and content, as things were going great for him. He loved his job, and the money was good. He found a great church to attend and loved the friendships that he had developed along the way. In short, he felt like he was living the dream, at least the one he had for back then.

Over the course of time, he started looking at things with a different perspective. Somewhere around the age of thirty-eight, he began to have an epiphany about his current situation and began to feel a shift. (Does this sound familiar?) He wasn't in panic mode or being driven by fear because of his age. He was simply beginning to dream about doing more with his life for the first time in a while. He also thought about eventually finding that special someone and settling down and having a family. He simply wanted more, so he did what every one of us does from time to time—he evaluated his progress according to his expectation of where he thought his life should be at that particular time.

After analyzing his current situation, working through his emotions, and navigating his thoughts, he made a decision to step toward his Next. He knew it wasn't too late for him, and he began to move forward, starting the process of making his dream a reality.

Sometimes the older we get, the more aware we are of the things that we've yet to accomplish. Those unfulfilled dreams and goals that we have tucked away begin to make their way back to the surface of our consciousness and begin to stare us in the face. Sometimes we react in panic or fear at the thought of never obtaining them. Shortly after that, the feeling can easily turn into hopelessness or despair. The attitude of how you respond has the potential to produce the results. You can have a feeling of being stuck and continue to settle in to a mediocre lifestyle, or you can choose to believe that your next step will start you on a wonderful journey of reaching your dreams in life.

As I sat there at lunch listening to my friend talk about his next step, I couldn't help but notice how excited he was about his future. I had never seen him this excited about anything except football! His every word was laced with passion and the utmost enthusiasm. He was glowing from head to toe and full of confidence as he shared his plan to move back to his hometown, finish school, and get the degree that he had always dreamed of. He knew exactly what he was going to do and how he was going to go about doing it. The type of degree he wanted would take about four years, but he accepted it; he was excited, nervous, and a little afraid all at the same time, but he was moving forward anyway. The main thing was that he had a plan.

Hector is now a couple of years into earning his degree and making tremendous progress. Just like Hector, there are many people who started toward their dream or goal later in life and still became a great success.

You Can Start at Any Time or Any Stage

Here's a list of a few people who started their journey later in life and went on to do great things.

- Anna Mary Robertson Moses, also known as Grandma Moses, was a famous artist who started her painting career at the age of seventy-eight. Her paintings have been displayed and sold all around the world; in 2006 one was sold for $1.2 million.

- Henry Ford was forty-five years old when he created the Model T car.
- Have you heard of Julia Child? If you've spent any time around the kitchen, then you know she is a famous celebrity chef. She wrote her very first cookbook at the age of fifty, which was the catalyst for her career as a television celebrity chef.

While I'm at it, I think it's pretty important to mention here that you're never *too young* to get started on doing something great in life.

- Bill Gates showed interest in computer programming at the age of thirteen. At the age of fifteen, he and his business partner developed a computer program that monitored traffic patterns in Seattle and made around $20,000 for their work.
- Tiger Woods started taking an interest in golf at the age of six months. He would watch his dad hit golf balls and try to mimic him. By the age of two, he made his first appearance on a television show, demonstrating his golf swing. By age five, he was featured in *Golf Digest* magazine. And today he's one of the top golfers in the world.

You are never too old or too young to begin living your dream. Start now and get after it!

Chapter 30

IN IT
TO WIN IT

ongratulations! I'm sure you are going through a range of
emotions right about now. I hope that you are excited about
the possibilities that are in store for you, but at the same
time I'm sure those feelings of excitement are accompanied by
some uncertainty.

Let me help you out here—it's perfectly okay if you are a little
nervous, scared, or even hesitant about whether or not you will
make it. What's not okay is you never taking that first initial step
to find out. You will never be 100 percent sure of anything. So,
if you're waiting for that 100-percent certainty, you will probably
miss out on all the opportunities that are out there with your name
on them. The only thing you need to be sure of is the very fact that
you are in it to win it.

Remember the words of John Wayne: "Courage is being scared
to death but saddling up anyway." It is very possible to be scared
and make progress all at the same time. No matter what, you just
have to keep moving forward.

The last thing I want to leave with you is a very sobering question—a question in which your answer will determine the outcome
of whether or not you will ever reach your Next. It's a question that

you can't ignore. It's a question that will not go away until you step up to the plate and respond to its continual beckoning. Here it is.

What Are You Going to Do Next?

Are you going to do what it takes to become the person you've been dreaming about? Are you going to take the necessary steps to move in the right direction for your life? Or will you sit there and come up with excuse after excuse as to why you haven't moved any closer to accomplishing your goals? Yes, I'm giving you a little tough love, but it's because I genuinely want you to succeed. It is my hope that after reading this book, you will be greatly encouraged and inspired to be the success you desire to be.

Your success is up to you. *It's always been up to you.* It's not up to your boss, family members, or friends. It's not up to chance or luck.

It's time to dig down deep to the core of who you are and find that inner strength and confidence that's been buried underneath the piles of debris and rubbish from your past failures and mistakes. You have to roll up your sleeves and get ready to put in the hard work that's required, because as we know, nothing great comes without work.

Are you ready to start putting into practice some of the things you've just read about in this book? Will you start applying some of the simple principles that I shared with you? If you're ready for change, then it's up to you to make it happen. It's time for you to step outside your comfort zone into the arena of possibilities beyond your wildest dreams. Remember, there is no magic formula or shortcut that will have you living your dream tomorrow, next week, or even next month. It's going to take a commitment and determination on your part to make your dreams a reality.

You will have to be committed enough to stay in the fight and stay the course.

There is no option for you to quit and throw in the towel. Quitting will get you more of what you already have, and you don't want to settle for that. Your determination will be the driving force that will get you through the hardships, setbacks, and difficult times that you will no doubt encounter on your journey toward your Next. Now you are ready to face them and reach for the life you've been dreaming about.

I want to share some final words of encouragement with you…

- I believe in you.

- I believe in your dream.

- I believe there is more in you than what you think.

- I believe you have what it takes to make those dreams your reality.

- I believe you are destined for more.

- I believe your decision to take a leap of faith will result in greatness.

- I believe your confidence will rise to a new level.

- I believe your fears will diminish as your determination grows stronger.

- I believe your next days will be your best days.

You have the power and the ability to decide today and start the amazing journey of going from where you are to where you want to be. All you have to do is *start*.

You've taken the time to read this book all the way to the last chapter. That says a lot about your ability to finish what you have started. Please don't forget what you've read or put it in the back of your mind for a more perfect time. *Now* is the time for you to put some of these principles and ideas into action.

Don't waste one more day wishing for your dreams to come to pass. Go out right now and start the ball rolling.

Here's one more next step for you. Grab a piece of paper and a pen and write out the following:

1. My dream/goal is:

2. One area that I will focus on that will increase my capacity:

3. One person I will connect with that I can learn from:

Whatever you do, *don't stay stuck*. Stay flexible instead, always looking for ways to move forward to your goals and dreams. Be creative. Be determined. And be empowered that you—and only you—can create the life you've always wanted.

So on your mark, get set, *go*! Your Next is just one step away.

ABOUT THE AUTHOR

Adonis Lenzy is a pastor, speaker, and communicator whose passion is inspiring others to live the life they have imagined. With more than twenty years of experience in both full-time ministry and public speaking, Adonis has developed a unique style of communicating in creative, illustrative, and humorous ways to people from all walks of life—crossing ethnic, denominational, and cultural barriers.

He's originally from San Antonio, Texas, and now resides in Nashville, Tennessee. He believes that nothing is more important than family, and he loves spending time with his wife, Heather, and his two children, Grayson and Kherington. He also enjoys golf, barbecue, and Southern-style sweet tea.

Whether speaking at conferences, organizations, church groups, or communicating through his writing, his message will no doubt inspire, motivate, and equip audiences for next-level living.

www.AdonisLenzy.com